First World War
and Army of Occupation
War Diary
France, Belgium and Germany

36 DIVISION
107 Infantry Brigade
Royal Irish Rifles
1st Battalion
1 February 1918 - 29 May 1919

WO95/2502/3

The Naval & Military Press Ltd
www.nmarchive.com
Published in association with The National Archives

Published by

The Naval & Military Press Ltd

Unit 10 Ridgewood Industrial Park,

Uckfield, East Sussex,

TN22 5QE England

Tel: +44 (0) 1825 749494

www.naval-military-press.com

www.nmarchive.com

This diary has been reprinted in facsimile from the original. Any imperfections are inevitably reproduced and the quality may fall short of modern type and cartographic standards.

© Crown Copyright
Images reproduced by permission of The National Archives, London, England, 2015.

Contents

Document type	Place/Title	Date From	Date To
Heading	WO95/2502/3		
Heading	36th Division 107th Infy Bde 1st Bn Roy. Irish Rif. Feb 1918-May 1919 From 8 Div 25 Bde		
Miscellaneous	Officers, Warrant Officers, Non-Commisiioned Officers, And Men Of The Royal Irish Rifles	19/12/1918	19/12/1918
Miscellaneous	Account By Lieut.-Colonel H.W.D. MacCarthy-O'Leary. D.S.O., M.C., (R. Irish Rifles) March 23rd And 24th 1918		
War Diary	In The Field	01/02/1918	28/02/1918
War Diary	Essigny	01/03/1918	17/03/1918
War Diary	Gd. Seracourt	18/03/1918	23/03/1918
War Diary	Beaumont En Beine	24/03/1918	24/03/1918
War Diary	Sermaize	25/03/1918	26/03/1918
War Diary	Erches	26/03/1918	27/03/1918
War Diary	Etacht 4. Erches	27/03/1918	28/03/1918
War Diary	Sourdon	28/03/1918	31/03/1918
Heading	107th Brigade. 36th Division. 1st Battalion Royal Irish Rifles April 1918		
War Diary	In The Field	01/04/1918	30/04/1918
War Diary	Wagram Fm	01/05/1918	06/05/1918
War Diary	Canal Bank	07/05/1918	10/05/1918
War Diary	Line	11/05/1918	16/05/1918
War Diary	Hospital Fm	17/05/1918	29/05/1918
War Diary	Canal Bk	30/05/1918	31/05/1918
War Diary	Line	01/06/1918	05/06/1918
War Diary	Road Camp	06/06/1918	13/06/1918
War Diary	Pekin Camp	15/06/1918	21/06/1918
War Diary	Tunnellers Camp	22/06/1918	22/06/1918
War Diary	Bois St Acaire	23/06/1918	30/06/1918
War Diary	In The Field (Tunnellers Camp)	01/07/1918	01/07/1918
War Diary	Tunnellers Camp	03/07/1918	03/07/1918
War Diary	St Marie Cappel	04/07/1918	04/07/1918
War Diary	Opelacre	06/07/1918	07/07/1918
War Diary	Line	07/07/1918	08/07/1918
War Diary	Millam	10/07/1918	10/07/1918
War Diary	Line	12/07/1918	31/07/1918
War Diary	In The Field (Support)	01/08/1918	31/08/1918
War Diary	Mont Noir Area (Berthen)	01/09/1918	01/09/1918
War Diary	Line (Support)	02/09/1918	04/09/1918
War Diary	Front Line	05/09/1918	08/09/1918
War Diary	Line	08/09/1918	12/09/1918
War Diary	Support	13/09/1918	15/09/1918
War Diary	Berthen	17/09/1918	19/09/1918
War Diary	Terdeghem	20/09/1918	20/09/1918
War Diary	Bissezeele	23/09/1918	26/09/1918
War Diary	Tunnelling Camp	27/09/1918	27/09/1918
War Diary	P Camp	28/09/1918	28/09/1918
War Diary	Ypres White Chateau	29/09/1918	29/09/1918
War Diary	Westhoek	30/09/1918	30/09/1918
War Diary	In Support	01/10/1918	01/10/1918

War Diary	In Line	02/10/1918	04/10/1918
War Diary	Terhand	05/10/1918	13/10/1918
War Diary	Support	14/10/1918	14/10/1918
War Diary	Line	14/10/1918	16/10/1918
War Diary	Rollinghem Cappel	18/10/1918	18/10/1918
War Diary	Lendelede	19/10/1918	19/10/1918
War Diary	Support	20/10/1918	20/10/1918
War Diary	Line	20/10/1918	23/10/1918
War Diary	Desselghem	24/10/1918	26/10/1918
War Diary	Lendelede	27/10/1918	27/10/1918
War Diary	Belleghem	29/10/1918	31/10/1918
Miscellaneous	36th Division	22/10/1918	22/10/1918
Miscellaneous	All Divisional Units	26/10/1918	26/10/1918
Miscellaneous	Major-General C. Coffin, V.C., D.S.O., Commanding 36th Division	22/10/1918	22/10/1918
War Diary	Belleghem	01/11/1918	01/11/1918
War Diary	Reckem Area	03/11/1918	03/11/1918
War Diary	Mouscron	04/11/1918	26/11/1918
Miscellaneous	The Officer Commanding 1st Bn The Royal Irish Rifles	23/12/1918	23/12/1918
War Diary	Mouscron	00/11/1918	00/11/1918
War Diary	Mouscron	07/12/1918	25/12/1918
War Diary	Mouscron	19/11/1918	19/11/1918
War Diary	Mouscron	18/12/1918	29/05/1919

N095/3500/3.

36TH DIVISION
107TH INFY BDE

1ST BN ROY. IRISH RIF.

FEB ~~JAN~~ 1918-MAY 1919

From. 8 DIV
25 Bde

OFFICERS, WARRANT OFFICERS, NON-COMMISIIONED OFFICERS,

AND MEN OF THE ROYAL IRISH RIFLES.

Since I last sent you a Christmas Greeting the British Army has emerged triumphantly from the supreme crisis of the war. It has never been put to a more searching test and it has never responded more magnificiently.

The greatest war in the history of the world has ended in the most complete victory for the British and Allied arms. The British Army has maintained its glorious reputation.

As your Colonel I have always watched with interest the doings of all the battalions of the Royal Irish Rifles and I am proud of the distinguished part they have played. They have maintained the fighting tradition of Irish Soldiers.

Some of you will shortly be returning to civil life. To these I wish God-speed and hope that the lesson of comradeship that you have learned in a great regiment in time of war will serve you in good stead all through life.

To those of you who remain in the Army I send warm greetings and hope that you will maintain in peace time the high standard you have attained in war.

Officers, Warrant Officers, Non-commissioned Officers and Men, I wish you all happiness in the coming year on the conclusion of your great task and the return of peace.

(sd) Henry Wilson General

19.12.18.   Colonel of The Royal Irish Rifles.

General Davies
For your retention, please.

COPY.

<u>Account by Lieut.-Colonel H.W.D. MacCarthy-O'Leary.</u>

D.S.O., M.C., (R.Irish Rifles)

<u>MARCH 23rd and 24th 1918.</u>

The morning of the 23rd March found both Battalions of the Royal Irish Rifles in the vicinity of Faucourt (square Q.12).

Shortly after midday both were ordered to Cugny (square R.20/26).

The 2nd Bn. Royal Irish Rifles proceded to occupy a defensive position E. and N.E. of the village astride the Cugny - Flavy le Martel Road. Another Battalion, belonging, I thought, to the 14th Division were on their right prolonging the position southwards.

The 1st Bn. Royal Irish Rifles under my command we held in readiness on the high ground south of Cugny in square R.26.

During the afternoon large bodies of Germans were observed collecting under trees in square R. 27 B and D.

The 1st Bn. had by this time occupied a position which I had selected.

To the best of my recollection, it was at about 3.45 p.m. that the enemy's advance commenced.

This was preceded by an intense machine gun bombardment which continued until the light began to fail.

About 4.30 p.m. large numbers of men belonging to the Battalion in front, to which I referred, commenced a somewhat disorderly withdrawal through the left of my Battalion. I went forward to find out what was happening and met the Colonel of this battalion being carried back on a stretcher in a dying condition. His men were now retiring hastily.

It was now dusk and getting dark quickly. The noise of musketry and German shouting and cheering was great. They had broken through on my left front (there being no troops left there to stop them) and were firing at us in enfilade at short range.

Shortly afterwards they charged us from the front and the left. They were in superior numbers and we were overrun. In the turmoil I was hit and knocked down. I shouted to all I saw to retire south along the road.

A few hundred yards back I was able to collect the majority of the Battalion.

I then decided to withdraw to the next high ground which was in the vicinity of Beaulieu (square Q.36).

On the outskirts of the village I met an Infantry Officer of another regiment and an Artillery officer. As I was the senior I gave instructions for a defensive position to be dug N.E. of the village.

The infantry officer, a Major, had about 250 men of his Bn. already in position.

His regiment was a North-country one (I thought the York and Lancaster Regiment belonging to or attached to the 14th Division. I understood that they were a Labour Bn. and at the time was under the impression that they were the Bn. that had withdrawn earlier from in front of Cugny).

The men had had no rest since the 20th and were very tired; however they fell to and before long had made passable a attempt at digging isolated holes.

About 2 a.m. the acting Bde. Major arrived with rations. He told me to move my Bn. in support of the 2nd Bn. Royal Irish Rifles who had been forced through

Cugny and were now astride the main Villeselve - Cugny road. I pointed out that we had consolidated an excellent position; that the men were 'done', and that I believed we would be of greater use where we were.

He returned to Bde. H.Q. in Velleselve.

Dawn was breaking when he came back with orders to move at once to a position astride the main road in square Q.30 B and D.

It was daylight before I was able to collect the Bn. but luckily a thick mist covered the ground and we were able to reach and consolidate, after a fashion, the position allotted to us (See Map).

Some French machine guns were in position on my right rear.

I do not know if the North Country Battalion was pushed further forward on my right. I did not see them and do not think they moved. When the mist lifted the German artillery got busy, and for some time the shelling in our vicinity was heavy. When it 'slacked down' we were subjected to intermittent shelling from either our own or French guns from the direction slightly East of Guiscard.

Little happened to my immediate front until early afternoon but on the left our troops from Eaucourt and Ollezy could be seen retiring.

About 1.30 p.m. large forces of Germans followed and after a long halt S.E. of Eaucourt continued their advance.

About the same time messengers from my right company brought word that the enemy had got in behind us through the woods on that flank and that the French machine gunners had retired.

I immediately sent word to the O.C. 2nd Bn. Royal Irish Rifles to withdraw at once, and that we would cover their retirement. I followed this message with another but doubt if the messages were ever received. Machine gun fire from the high ground south of Cugny had now become heavy. The Germans were known to be behind us on our right while on our left at a distance of about 300 yards they were in strong force and had commenced to fire at us in enfilade.

At this point I gave the order to withdraw. The Bn. formed up south of the cross roads in square Q.30.c.

Hearing heavy firing from Beaumont en Beine (square W.6) and from the N.W. of Villeselve, I decided to retire still further and to get in touch with other units of the 36th Division. Marching through Villeselve a Colonial Cavalry officer - dressed as a Lt.-Colonel - stopped us. He told me he was a Brigadier and being a Cavalryman suggested that I should help him regarding the infantry dispositions. He showed me on his map where many other units of the 36th and 14th Divisions were. I then placed my Battalion in position facing N.W. in square Q.34 and rejoined him in the village.

Meanwhile other Battalions commenced to fall back and I assisted this officer in sending them to various positions. Later Lt.-Col. M.J. Furnell (C.O. 1st Royal Irish Fusiliers) joined me.

The village was now being heavily shelled. was

It was reported that Golancourt on our left in the enemy's hands and that he was south of Beaumont on our right.

A Lt.-Colonel on the staff suddenly appeared on the scene.

We debated whether we should retire and decided to issue orders for the move back to the high ground near Guiscard. The troops however did not wait for orders and fell back in confusion through the village.

Two officers went ahead in an ambulance and formed up the remnants of the Division as far as possible by units. The Royal Inniskilling and Irish Fusiliers on the south side of the road, the Royal Irish Rifles and other troops on the north of the road in square W.9.a.

We formed up in quarter column with a screen of cavalry in front facing Villeselve. Two flights of hostile aeroplanes circled round us for some time.

They did not fire at us nor did they direct any artillery fire against us.

It was now about 4 p.m. Brigadier-General W.F. Hessey (Commanding 109th Inf. Bde 36th Div.) arrived as we were forming up and ordered us to withdraw. I understood that the French were in position on the high ground East and West of Guiscard. Gun detachments (Pompoms) of their troops covered our retirement through Berlancourt. I now had charge of all Royal Irish Riflemen that I could gather.

The high ground (W.19) was occupied by our infantry. There were also French troops and several batteries of French artillery. It was getting dusk when I reached the outskirts of Guiscard and not meeting anyone of authority I placed the Royal Irish Rifles under cover of a quarry in square V.24.d. and went into the village to look for Bde H.Q. which was said to be here.

I was returning from a fruitless search when a staff officer of the 36th Division came galloping down the street. He told me that everyone had gone further back (in a southerly direction) and thought I should do likewise.

The place was now being heavily shelled so I moved as soon as possible and together with the French artillery set out in darkness along the Noyon road.

Some two miles further back an officer of the 36th Division had been posted to guide us to where the division was re-forming. This was another 2 or 3 miles further back. It is off the map and I do not recollect its name.

       (sd) H.W.D. MACCARTHY-O'LEARY,

            Lt.-Col.

1st Bn. THE ROYAL IRISH RIFLES.

WAR DIARY

INTELLIGENCE SUMMARY

February 1918

1st Bn. R. IR. RIFLES.

Place	Date	Hour	Summary of Events and Information	Remarks and references to Appendices
In the Field	1st		Battalion in billets in the Natoy Area.	
	2nd		Orders re transfer to the 36th (Ulster) Division received.	
	3rd		Battalion left the 87th Division entraining at HOPOUTRE.	
	4th		Detained at HAM and marched to billets in CUGNY.	
	5th		In billets at CUGNY.	
	6th		— do — 8 Officers & 200 Other Ranks transferred from 9/Bn.	
	7th		— do —	
	8th		Relieved 9th Bn. R.Ir. Rif. in Brigade Support.	
	9th		Relieved 15th Bn. in the Line — Bn. H.Q. at BRUSLES.	
	10th		1 O.R. Killed	
	11th		2 O.R. Wounded	
	12th		3 O.R. Wounded	
	15th		Relieved by 15th Bn. Royal Innishilling Fus: Moved to Argenz at ESSIGNY Station on Divisional Reserve.	
	16th		ESSIGNY — Worked on the Battle Zone G Sector. Capt Kearns, Lieut Colles and 5th O.R. joined Bn. 2nd Lieuts Miller & Gillespie struck off strength.	
	17th		ESSIGNY — Worked on the Battle Zone G Sector. Lieut Galloway struck off strength.	
	18th		— do —	
	19th		— do —	
	20th		— do — 2nd Lieut Nolan struck off strength	
	21st		— do —	
	22nd		Moved to the Quarries — Bn HQ at GRAND SERAUCOURT. Work on Battle Zone F Sector.	

1st Bn. THE ROYAL IRISH RIFLES.

WAR DIARY

INTELLIGENCE SUMMARY

(Erase heading not required.)

Army Form C. 2118.

February 1918 (Contd)

Place	Date	Hour	Summary of Events and Information	Remarks and references to Appendices
In the Field	2nd		Battalion and 1st Line Transport inspected by Major General O.S.W. Nugent C.B. D.S.O. L.O.C. 36th Division. Draft of 35 O.R. joined Bn: C.S.M Plummer to England (Commission)	
	25th		Moved into the Line in relief of 15th Bn R.Ir. Rifles. – Bn HQ at the Quarries.	

R Paton
Captain
Adjutant 1st Bn The Royal Irish Rifles.

3/3/18

1st Batt
R. Irish Rif.

WAR DIARY
INTELLIGENCE SUMMARY.
(Erase heading not required.)

Army Form C. 2118.

March 1918

Place	Date	Hour	Summary of Events and Information	Remarks and references to Appendices
ESSIGNY	7th	8.20 p.m.	Enemy Raid: At 8.20 p.m. a heavy Trench Mortar and Artillery barrage was put on AUVERGNE Trench (B.15.a, B.9.c, B.15.B.). Bombardment lasted about 20 minutes and then lifted to further in rear. Sentries in St BRUNO Trench (B.9.c.) saw a large body of the enemy crawling under, and in some cases, lifting and cutting our wire. They immediately opened fire and thin in near the junction of AUVERGNE Trench and St BRUNO Sap. Heavy rifle and Lewis gun fire was kept up on the enemy for about ten minutes. A few minutes afterwards, while intermittent fire was being kept up, a few bombs were thrown into the post at AUVERGNE Trench from the rear, and a large party of the enemy, numbering about 80, were seen in the rear of AUVERGNE Trench. They made for our throwing bombs, one of which fell on the Lewis gun and broke it in two pieces. The officer in command of the Platoon (B. H.D. SINCLAIR) was severely wounded, man was killed and 4 O.R. wounded. The parados was too high for the men to use their rifles and, after throwing at least 80 bombs, they retired RIGHT and LEFT down the trench. The raiders then entered the trench and threw bombs into dugouts. The Lance Corporal in charge of the Lewis gun, who was last seen standing beside his gun, is missing. The enemy left no dead unwounded, but it is certain he suffered heavy casualties. Working parties. 1 O.R. wounded. Working parties on front posts.	2

2 K.
3 M.

WAR DIARY

INTELLIGENCE SUMMARY

Army Form C. 2118.

Place	Date	Hour	Summary of Events and Information	Remarks and references to Appendices
ESSIGNY	4th		2 O.R. wounded.	
	5th		In front line trenches. 7 O.R. wounded.	
	6th		Battalion relieved by 12th (S) Bn. Royal Irish Rifles. proceeded by march route to billets. Bn. H.Q. in GRAND SERAUCOURT, "A" Coy. in HAMEL, "C" Coy in SOMME Dugouts, "B" and "D" Coys. in GRAND SERAUCOURT. 1 O.R. wounded.	
	7th		Cleaning kits and refitting. 2 O.R. posted to Coys.	
	8th		Training. 7 O.R. from 8/9 on reporting posted to Companies.	
	9th		Training. 8 O.R. Reinforcements posted to Companies.	
	10th		Training. 26 O.R. on joining unit posted to Companies.	
	11/12		Training.	
	13		Batt. relieved 15th (S) Bn. Royal Irish Rifles in the Battle Zone at Quarries in front of GRAND SERAUCOURT. Bn. H.Q. remained at Gd. SERAUCOURT, handing over to the 2nd Bn. R.Ir. Rifles.	
	14th		Work on Battle Zone. Usual training in the morning.	
	15th		Working parties. 2nd Lt. F.C. GUNNELL struck off strength on proceeding to England for 6 months.	
	16		Working parties in Battle Zone. 12 O.R. posted to Companies.	
	17		ST PATRICK'S DAY - observed as a holiday. 1st and 2nd Battalions united at Mass by Rev. F. GILL D.S.O. M.C.; first time since 1854. Football match in morning. 1st Bttn. 2 goals. 2nd Bn. 1 goal. Teams: Goal, Cpl. DIXON; Backs, Rfn. RUSHEAD, Sgt. STILES; Halves, CONROY, MEREDITH, L/C. CONVERY; Forwards, Lt. KERR, Rfn. SPENCE, L/C. BARR, Cpl. MALONE, Rfn. McADAMS. Battalion Sports in afternoon. Battn. won open Cookers (2). Competition in event open to whole II Army, near HAM.	

Army Form C. 2118.

WAR DIARY
INTELLIGENCE SUMMARY.
(Erase heading not required).

Instructions regarding War Diaries and Intelligence Summaries are contained in F. S. Regs., Part II. and the Staff Manual respectively. Title pages will be prepared in manuscript.

Place	Date	Hour	Summary of Events and Information	Remarks and references to Appendices
Q. SERAUCOURT	18		Work in Battle Zone.	
	19		Work on Battle Zone and Cable laying near BRAY St CHRISTOPHER.	
	20	8 p.m.	2nd Lt. E.J.P. STAPLETON struck off strength (Sick). Companies at work on trenches in Battle Zone and at ARTEMPS. Bn. Headquarters moved from the village to Battle Dugouts in the Quarries.	
	21	4.30 a.m.	German Offensive expected to open the coming morning – Information received from prisoners. Heavy bombardment of Battle Zone, front line Redoubts & gun positions by Artillery of all calibres. Gas shell extensively used. "A" Coy (Capt. REED M.C.) Battle Position being	
			Received it 4.40 a.m. "A" Coy (Capt. REED M.C.) Battle Position being Trenches, "B" Coy. (Capt. BROWN M.C.) occupied Battle Zone Trenches RIGHT; "D" Coy. (Capt. BAYLY) Redoubts right of Bn. H.Q. "C" Coy. (Lt. KERR) Counter Attack	2.3 Kilos
		12.30 p.m.	Intense shelling of Battle Zone developed about 9 a.m., particularly B & C Coy trenches, the Battalion being on all day until ordered to retire on HAMEL about 11 p.m.	
			Capt. J. BROWNE, M.C. wounded missing; Lt. J. KERR - P. OKANE - B.T. HODGSON, 2nd Lt. J.C. THOMPSON Killed. 2nd Lt. H. OLIVER - T.A. VALENTINE - J. AIKEN. Wounded.	2.3 Kilos
	22		Position taken up at HAMEL. Right flank on SOMME BANK. Large bodies of enemy and transport seen moving S. along St QUENTIN – St SIMON ROAD. Battalion engaged until ordered to fall back to Position near HAPPENCOURT, where it hung on till dusk, when the right flank being seriously threatened, orders were received to retire on the line SOMMETTE EAUCOURT — CUGNY behind the CANAL. Battalion moved across country crossing the Canal at PITHON by the Light Railway Bridge and proceeded to billets at EAUCOURT arriving 3 a.m.	12.8 Kilos
	23	6 a.m.	Heavy ground mist – Picquets sent out round the village. About 10 a.m. the village was shelled with 5.9 guns and the Battn moved out N.W. and dug in. Heavy fighting heard in the direction of HAM and ESMERT HALLON. 11.30 a.m. orders received to move to and occupy High	15.1 Kilos

WAR DIARY
or
INTELLIGENCE SUMMARY.
(Erase heading not required.)

Army Form C. 2118.

Place	Date	Hour	Summary of Events and Information	Remarks and references to Appendices
	23	3 p.m.	ground S. of CUGNY. Britan being EAST and CUGNY. Arrived about 3 p.m. in Britan being EAST and CUGNY. Got in touch with FRENCH (6th Dragoons) on RIGHT and 14th Division on LEFT. Enemy proceeded to rapidly advance on opposite height and an engagement ensued lasting until 11 p.m. when 14th Division on left falling back and GLOUCESTER ENTRENCHING BATN on RIGHT retiring, the line was pushed by the enemy and the Commanding Officer ordered a retirement on BEAUMONT, where the Bn. reassembled about 1 a.m. and dug in.	Lat. & Long. 15.1 + 160.3 15.9
		10 p.m.	2/Lt W.N. McNEIL. Lt Col. McCARTHY O'LEARY, D.S.O., M.C. wounded. Lt. remained in Command of Battn. Enemy patrol encountered in getting round our LEFT flank. Bn. H.Q. in Sunken Road pushed. The casualties.	1-5 K/Gen
BEAUMONT EN BEINE	24	4 a.m.	Battn. marched to MONTEILMONT on CUGNY - VILLERSELVE Road and dug in S. of the road and 700 yards in rear of the 2nd Battalion, British taken up previous night. B.H.Q. and that of 10th R.B. Rifle Brigade in Sunken road (10th R.B.) in trenches to right of ours and N. of same. A general engagement ensued up, large reinforcements approaching down road were shelly shelled in village about 10 a.m. FRENCH on right on wooded height near BEAUMONT retired and 30th Division	1-9 KILOS
		3 p.m.	Mount EAUCOURT. The Battn. remained, messages (3) being sent to 2nd Bn. to retire through us at 3 p.m. to general being received from 2nd Battn. 105 R.Bs. were ordered to retire. Runners sent to 2nd L.N. Lks were wounded.	
		3.30 p.m.	At 3.30 p.m. the Battn. was practically surrounded and had to retire on VILLERSELVE, where a defensive position N.W. of the village was taken up. Lt. Col. McCARTHY O'LEARY, D.S.O., M.C. being appointed O/C. troops. The 9th R. INNISKILLING FUSILIERS were seen to counter-attack the enemy who were approaching rapidly in large numbers. From this point two large columns of troops appears in columns of route were seen retiring the Canal N. of CUGNY. The latter troops proved part of 1st BAVARIAN DIV. 10th Div. 34th 37th Divisions.	
SERMAIZE	25th	3 a.m.	The covering British was held until 8.30 p.m. when the Battn. retired through GUISCARD S. MARTIN BUSSY to SERMAIZE near NOYON, where the Brigade came under the orders of G.O.C. Commanding FRENCH ARMY.	17.6 KILOS 42.10 KILOS

A8834 Wt.W4973 M687 759000 8/16 D. D. & L. Ltd. Forms/C.2118/13.

WAR DIARY
or
INTELLIGENCE SUMMARY
(Erase heading not required.)

Army Form C. 2118.

Place	Date	Hour	Summary of Events and Information	Remarks and references to Appendices
			(As the troops moved back large columns of French guns going up to the firing line went present and bivouacked for the night.	42.0 KILOS
	26	At 9 a.m.	the Battalion moved via GREDENVILLE to AVRICOURT (meeting the Transport) 12 noon, where it bivouaced to bivouack. At 2 p.m. it moved off via BEUVRAIGNES - TILLOLOY - GRIVILLERS - MARQUIVILLERS to GUERBIGNY, arriving 12 m. 26th BRIGADE H.Q. in the town	33.5
		10 a.m.	The Battalion moved out of the town and manned a position 2 miles to the EAST. N. of the river AVRE, Lt.Col. MACCARTHY O'LEARY being placed in command of a group:- 1st Royal Irish Rifles	3.5
		5 p.m.	2nd Royal Irish Rifles under Capt. MURPHY, 15th R.I. Rifles under Capt. MILLER.
ERCHES		At 5 p.m.	a trench position was occupied 700 yards W. of village of ERCHES. 2nd R.I. Rif. on right; 1st R.I.R. centre; 15th R.I. Rif. left. The Battalion was posted in old French trenches and dugouts and old ammunition dumps along the BOUCHOIR - GUERBIGNY road. French dismounted Cavalry were withdrawn and the 109th Infy. Bde. on our quarter right front being in action.
		About 10 p.m.,	the enemy, 1st GUARDS DIVISION approached the village, bearing lights by use of French uniform. They kidnapped in on our unsuspecting in our case the occupants. Desultory fire opened which last developed into bursts of M.G. fire of some intensity. Having made good the village, light trench mortars were brought up and our positions bombarded. On two occasions the white flag was used to distract attention whilst machine guns crews operated on the other's flank and considerable use made of the presumed ignorance of FRENCH viz:- "Dont fire we are French", until it became necessary to warn the troops to fire on all in front. At dawn, 5.9 guns being brought up, the companies on the gun pits were driven out at point blank range. and a charge was made on the enemy, who rapidly retired, thus enabling the Battalion to withdraw fighting. The Commanding Officer being wounded about this time, he was evacuated and the retirement fighting commenced.	MAP REF. SHEET 66.70000
	27	2 a.m.	At 2 a.m. the Commanding Officer ordered 2/Lt. FENNEL, Intelligence Officer, M.O. Lt. CAMERON to order the Nissen staff to proceed along main road to AVRILLERS. They proceeded through HANGEST - PLESSIER - ROSAINVILLERS - LEHAMEL - PIERREPONT - HARGICOURT - AUBVILLERS to SAUVILLERS	

WAR DIARY or INTELLIGENCE SUMMARY

Army Form C. 2118.

Place	Date	Hour	Summary of Events and Information	Remarks and references to Appendices
			arriving 5 p.m. Same date.	7/9 K1-22
	27th 28th		Capt. TAYLER'S party left about 4.45 a.m. to 107th Fd. Hos. at Q.2.8.2.9, then joined by Asst Adjutant 1/Lt. LEEPER, 2/Lt. GREEN and 16 specialists,/advanced with two German P.W. Lt. DAVENSCOURT, CONTOIRE-PIERREPONT-HARGICOURT-MALPART-GRIVESNES, arriving 2/0 m joining transport, proceeding forthwith to SAUVILLERS where party (?) was met. 10a.m. 28th/parties 1 and 2 moved to SOURDON.	21-6 -- 5.3
GTACHT 4. ERCHES		10.15a.m.	2/ Capt. H.R. REED, Capt. R.O.H. LAW, M.C., 2/Lt. I.J. O'SULLIVAN, Lt. E.R.B. COLLIS, 2/Lt. I.H. TURKINGTON, 1/Lt. FARLEY and 98 men being driven off the gun pits at 10-15 a.m. retired to a position Q.2.a. central - Q.3.2.4.8, fighting a rearguard action. On receipt of orders a further position S. of HANGEST J.30. a. 3.0. to J.30.a.8.5 was taken. The French retired the same day and the party marched SOURDON via HANGEST-PLESSIER ROSAINVILLERS-MOREUIL-MAILLY	
	27th 28th	10 a.m.	Lt. Col. H.W.D. MACCARTHY O'LEARY, D.S.O., M.C., Lt. E.Y. MANICO, 2/Lt. T. ENRIGHT, 2/Lt. R. MOORE, M.M. and 2/Lt. F.W. HOYLE wounded.	
			4/ Capt. E. PATTON (Adjutant), A/Capt. L.M. BAYLY, 2/Lt.T.H.R. BROWNE and 68 O.R. on retiring drew in on a position K.26. b.5.0. - K.26.2.9.9. and remained fighting all night. On July 28 at 11 a.m. 25% marched E. of HANGEST via FRESNOY - MEZIERES - VILLERSAUX - ERABLES - MOREUIL - MAILLY to SOURDON arriving 7 p.m.	7.4
SOURDON	28		Detachment 1.2.3 (Strength 115 O.R.) moved from SOURDON at 1.30 p.m. via ERCLAINVILLERS to GOULLEMELLE where they lay in on E. of village T.10.a. Central to T.10.c.3.0. and manned their posts during the night.	
	29	4 a.m.	An attack from hostile forces located at MESNIL ST. GEORGES, W. of MONTDIDIER being anticipated at 4 a.m. (29th) a party of 20 men under Capt. H. TAYLER was sent to locate enemy in VILLERS TOURNELLE; finding same unoccupied the party moved on to CANTIGNY and having located French troops returned.	
		2.6 p.m.	The Brigade moved off via FOLLEVILLE to CHAUSSOY EPARGNY, arriving at 5 p.m. and mustering	1/3 3

WAR DIARY
or
INTELLIGENCE SUMMARY.
(Erase heading not required.)

Army Form C. 2118.

Place	Date	Hour	Summary of Events and Information	Remarks and references to Appendices
	30		Attachment to unit Capt. BAYLY which has arrived from SOURDON via CHIRMONT.	113.5 N606 14.2 K160
		7p.m.	At 7p.m. the Battalion paraded and moved on to VARENNES via BERNY-JUMEL. ORESMAUX - LEULLY to near POIX arriving at 4 a.m. 30th were billets were occupied. The Battalion rested until 4 p.m. when it proceeded by march route via TAISNIL to SAISUX railhead. 8 of AMIENS arriving at 11/30 p.m. and entrained on the rendéon.	24.4 — — 16.8 — —
			During these operations the following casualties occurred :- 31 O.R. Killed. 248 wounded. 155 missing - 9 wounded and missing - a total of 439.	188.9 N608
	31	8 a.m.	Train entrained for GAMACHES. Arrived 1 p.m. and proceeded by march route to billets. Transport at HOCQULUST. Companies at FRETTMEUL, SAXTON-VICQ. at MONCHELET.	

Atherd.
Lieut-Col.
O.C.
Comdg. 1st Bn. The Royal Irish Rifles.

107th Brigade.
36th Division.

1st BATTALION

ROYAL IRISH RIFLES

APRIL 1918.

1st Battn.
R. Irish Rifles 107/36
Vol 4 3

Army Form C. 2118

WAR DIARY
INTELLIGENCE SUMMARY.
(Erase heading not required.)

April 1918.

Instructions regarding War Diaries and Intelligence Summaries are contained in F. S. Regs., Part II. and the Staff Manual respectively. Title pages will be prepared in manuscript.

Place	Date	Hour	Summary of Events and Information	Remarks and references to Appendices
In the Field	April 1st		The Battn. entrained about 8am at SALEUX Rail.head. S of AMIENS. detrained about 1pm at GIMACHES near TRÉPORT. Proceeded by march route to G.H.Q. Troops at HOOQULUST. Companies at FRETMEUH BHQ at MONTLICHER.	
	2nd		Draft of 160 men of 10th & 13th Bn Royal Irish Rifles & 4 Officers. Capt. W.R. Bell. 2/Lt F.H. Lewis. 2/Lt F.N. CULLEN 2/Lt E.L. BEATTY arrived. Views taken on Route of Battn. & Rfm. COEN (Y/S390) proceed S/S 78 as en route England on munitions.	
	3rd		Battn. entrained at FOUQUIÈRES at 3pm. on Tactical Train. 25 officers & 66 O.R.	
	4th		Battn. detrained 1am. - Proceeded by Lorry to No 6 SEIGE Camp. near BRIELEN. for refitting.	
	5th		MAJOR T.H. IVEY assumed command of Battn. Refitting & Baths.	
	6th		2/Lt H. DEVINE & 2/Lt W. McPHERSON reported on posting. 3 OR. CAPT. G.H.P. WHITFELD proceeded England S/0 10th R.A.F. Battn. relieved 2 Bn South Wales Borderers & 2 Welch Regt. (1st DIVISION) in LANGEMARK. POELCAPPEL Trenches BHQ at HUBNER. 1 OR wounded.	
	7th			
	8th		2/Lt W.E. PARKE 10th B.A. on posting reported at Detail Camp Hospital Farm TRIANGLE CAMP. 1 OR accidentally wounded.	
	9th		Lieut. R.C. McCRUM & 30 OR joined on posting. 1 OR accidentally wounded.	
	10th		24 OR on posting from 10th & 14th Bn The Royal Irish Rifles reported their posts to 15548.	
	2d		150 OR relief 11th B. Composite 14 Rl. Rfles moved by Light Railway Hospital Farm Mysi Batt in the line. 1 OR Killed. 2 OR wounded.	
	11th		Draft of D1 O.R. on joining were posted to Companies. 1 OR accidentally injured.	

Army Form C. 2118.

WAR DIARY
or
INTELLIGENCE SUMMARY.
(Erase heading not required)

Instructions regarding War Diaries and Intelligence Summaries are contained in F.S. Regs., Part II. and the Staff Manual respectively. Title pages will be prepared in manuscript.

1st BN. THE ROYAL IRISH RIFLES.

Officer i/c Adjutant.

Place	Date	Hour	Summary of Events and Information	Remarks and references to Appendices
In Field	12 April		160 O.R. from Ireland taken on strength of Battⁿ	
	14ᵗʰ		150 Lieu. Tempany attached returned to unit, 17ᵗʰ Battⁿ R.I. Rfles.	
	15ᵗʰ		8 O.R. from 23ʳᵈ Entrenching Battⁿ. employed at 7ᵗʰ Jan. H.Q. Taken on strength of Battⁿ. Battⁿ. moved to PILKEM LINE. B.H.Q. MORTELJE FARM.	
	17ᵗʰ		2nd Lt — wounded. 2/Lt. T. Farley & 2/Lt. H. Devine. wounded.	
	18ᵗʰ		1 O.R. missing. 1 O.R. in Base wastage.	
	19ᵗʰ		3 O.R. wounded. Battⁿ moved to CANAL BANK.	
	20ᵗʰ		3 O.R. Killed. 6 wounded. Lt Colonel J.R. Henri, D.S.O. R.E. M. accompanied command of 7ᵗʰ Battⁿ.	
	21ˢᵗ		Battⁿ returned from CANAL BANK — occupied no 6 Camp — relieving 2nd Bn R.I. Rifles. 2. OR. Struck off strength. Lt. A.J.M. Ren. Struck off strength. Lⁿ General. O. S. W. NUGENT, C.B. R.I.R. Killed — addressed 1st Battalion.	
	22ⁿᵈ		Battⁿ moved into PILKEM Trenches. B.H.Q. FOCH FARM. Relieving 11ᵗʰ Bn & 2L Royal Irish Rifles.	
	24ᵗʰ		1 OR joined. 2/Lts Macauley. 2/Lt. J.R.H. Macauley / Royal Dublin Fusiliers. on reporting joined unit.	
	28ᵗʰ		2/L. P/ CULLEN. 2/Lt. J.J. Dolan. 2/Lt. T.C. HAIGH. 2Lt. J. McKenna Royal Dublin Fusiliers on posted joined 1st Regiment. 2/Lt. R. Murphy. 4 1ˢᵗ R. I. R. reported / joined 1st unit.	
	27ᵗʰ		3 OR wounded	
	28ᵗʰ		2/Lt. W.J. LINTON. 10th Bn R. Rfles on posting joined 1st Regiment. 10. OR wounded	
	29ᵗʰ		2/Lt. H.C. GREEN. Middlˣ Fusil. Killed. 4 F.B. COLLES wounded. 2/Lt. F.H. Lewis. Killed. 2 O.R. joint.	
	30ᵗʰ		7 Killed 5 OR missing. MAJOR J.A. MULHOLLAND. M.C. on posting R.I.R. assumed duties of 2ⁿᵈ i/c command.	

6538 F.W. W8957 M.683 E.V5 A.OOO 8/16 D.D. & L.Ltd. Forms/C.2118/13.

1st R. Irish Rifle.

Army Form C. 2118.

WAR DIARY
or
INTELLIGENCE SUMMARY.

(Erase heading not required.)

MAY, 1918.

WO 4[...]

Place	Date	Hour	Summary of Events and Information	Remarks and references to Appendices
WAGRAM FM.	1st.		2 Companies in huts. 2 Companies in trenches. 1 OR to Base "infit".	
	2nd		Working in trenches at Wagram Fm.	
	3rd		Training & digging.	
	4th		Do. 1 OR to Base "underage".	
	5		Do.	
	6.		Do. 1 OR " for employment. 3 OR to Base "underage".	
CANAL BANK	7		Proceeded to Canal Bank. 14 OR joined Bn.	
	8		1 OR joined Bn. 1 OR killed. 6 OR wounded (1 OR died of wounds)	
	10		Enemy shelled Canal Bank in the evening.	
			Bn. moved into left sub-section. 2 OR joined Bn. 4 OR wounded. 1 OR to Base "infit".	
LINE	11		5 OR killed. 4 OR wounded. (1 Died of Wounds.) 8 OR joined Bn. 55 OR posted to Bn. from 2½ Garr. Bn.	
	12.		1 OR killed. 3 OR wounded. 10 OR wounded & shell shock.	
	13		4 OR wounded.	
	14.		1 OR wounded. 10 OR joined Bn. from 12 Bn. 10 OR joined Bn. from 16 Bn. 10 OR transferred to 15 Bn.	
	15.		1 OR joined Bn. from T.M.B. 10 OR joined Bn. from Div. Wing.	
	16.		2 OR wounded. Bn. relieved by 12/Bn. and moved to HOSPITAL FARM.	
HOSPITAL FM.	17.		Cleaning up and refitting	
	18.		Training & recreation	
	19.		Working on "Green Line". 4 OR joined Bn.	
	20.		Do. Working on Green Line. Football (intercompany)	
	21.		10 OR joined Bn. Training.	
	22.		2 " transferred from Div. Wing. working on Green Line.	
	24.		1 " transferred to 12/Bn. Do.	
	25.		Training.	

Army Form C. 2118.

MAY 1918.

WAR DIARY
or
INTELLIGENCE SUMMARY.
(Erase heading not required.)

Place	Date	Hour	Summary of Events and Information	Remarks and references to Appendices
HOSPITAL FM.	26th		19 OR. joined Bn from Divis. Wing. 10 OR. joined from 8th Div. T.M.B. 10th/Divis. formed 233rd Emp. Coy. 1 OR. Taken on estab. of T.M.B. Final Football Competition.	
	27th		Cricket match with R.G.A.	
	28.		Capt. M. Forbes. Lt. D.J. McCullough. MC. Lt. J.S. Bragford taken on strength.	
	29.		Bn. proceeded to Supports. HdQrs. CANAL BANK, relieving 12/Bn.	
CANAL BK.	30.		1 OR. killed. 10 OR. buried by shell. Major Ja. Mulholland. M.C. injured from hospital	
	31.		1 OR. reported to 2nd. Bn. Working in Bde. Support. Trenches.	

Honours + Awards.

Bar to M.C. Capt. R.O.H. LAW. M.C.
" " Lt. E. PATTON. M.C.

Military Cross: Capt. L.M. BAYLY.

D.C.M. 9661. C.S.M. BAINES.
20156. Sgt. DOHERTY.

M.M.
10225. L/C. KEELING.
20428. Rfn. RILEY.

[signed] Jackson Capt.
[stamp] 10th BN. THE ROYAL IRISH RIFLES.

1 R Irish Regt
June 1918

WAR DIARY
INTELLIGENCE SUMMARY
(Erase heading not required.)

Army Form C. 2118.

ORDERLY ROOM
No. 1451

Instructions regarding War Diaries and Intelligence Summaries are contained in F.S. Regs., Part II and the Staff Manual respectively. Title pages, I.R.

Place	Date	Hour	Summary of Events and Information	Remarks and references to Appendices
LINE	1st		Battn in the Line in Left Subsector — Battn Headquarters at HILL TOP MINE. 1 OR wounded.	
	2nd		1 O.R. wounded.	
	3rd		2 O.R. wounded (1 Accidental)	
	4th		2 O.R. wounded (1 Accidental); 1 OR struck off strength: 2 OR to Base (1 unfit for undercarriage)	
	5th		2 O.R. wounded. Battn relieved on night of 5/6 by 3/1 Grenadier Regt (Belgian Army) and moved by rail from READING to ROAD CAMP (near ST JAN DER BIEZEN) for training.	
ROAD CAMP	6th		Battn cleaning up and refitting; 1 OR wounded (attached 107th M.B.)	
	7th		Baths and inspections. Lecture by G.S.O.1.	
	8th		Reorganization; 41 OR joined Battn from II Corps Jeupy Works Bn and 4 OR from 36th Divisional Reception Camp.	
	9th		Reorganization; 1 OR to England for Commission. Officers of the Battn were inspected by Lieut-General Sir Claud Jacob KCB Commdg II Army Corps.	
	10th		107th Infantry Brigade also inspected by Corps Commander	
	12th		2 OR transferred to 1st Bn Royal Irish Rifles	
	13th		The Battn moved by road to PEKIN CAMP relieving 1st Royal Irish Fusiliers. Battn working on EAST POPERINGHE LINE; 2 Lieuts McMahon, MacFaffiko & A.A.L.McManus joined Battn; 4 OR joined Duc Wing; 1 OR joined Battn from I Expdy Wks Battn	
PEKIN CAMP	15th		1 OR to Base undercarriage	
	16th		1 OR to Base undercarriage. 3 OR joined 36th Divisional Reception Camp: CSM Carmichael proceeded to U.K. for temporary Commission	

Army Form C. 2118.

WAR DIARY
INTELLIGENCE SUMMARY
(Erase heading not required.)

June 1918 (contd)

Place	Date	Hour	Summary of Events and Information	Remarks and references to Appendices
PEKIN CAMP	18th		1 OR died in Hospital (Bruxia); 3 OR (ASC) taken on strength; Lieut. H.B. McConnell proceeded to 111 G.Corps, GRANTHAM	
	19th		Capt. Schroeder 6D & Lieut. Legg taken on strength of Batt.	
	21st		1 OR to Base from 36G Divisional Reception Camp.	
TUNNELLERS CAMP	22nd		1 OR joined Div. Reception Camp. Batt. moved by road to TUNNELLERS Camp.	
BOIS ST ACAIRE	23rd		Batt. moved at 3.0 p.m. to Bois St Acaire Musketry Camp	
	24th		Batt. on Range.	
	25th		Batt. on Range; 1 OR to England for Commission; 15 OR rejoined Bn. from N Res Batt.	
	26th		Lieut. McGarrivier taken on strength	
	27th		Batt. sports held — winners "A" Company	
	28th		Interplatoon Musketry Competition held; Winner 16 Platoon; Officers of Batt. played the 153rd Bde R.F.A. at Rugby at HOUTKERQUE winning 3 to nil; 10 OR transferred from 2nd Bn R.I.Rif.	
	30th		Batt. moved to TUNNELLERS Camp by road. 10 OR joined Batt. from Reception Camp.	

Honours and Awards

DSO. Capt. J.H. Loog
Mentioned in Dispatches 7.4.18. Capt. H. Loog; Capt. & QM. W. Edwards.
7146 RQMS Corrigan; 7274 LSgt Niven; 11920 LSgt Holmes.

Mentioned Service Medal 7146 RQMS Corrigan; 7274 LSgt Niven; 11920 LSgt Holmes.

[signature]
ADJUTANT
2nd BN. THE ROYAL IRISH RIFLES

Army Form C. 2118.

WAR DIARY
or
INTELLIGENCE SUMMARY.
(Erase heading not required.)

PAGE 1.

Place	Date	Hour	Summary of Events and Information	Remarks and references to Appendices
In the Field (Charlton Camp)	July 18 1st.		The 36th (Ulster) Division horse show was held at PROVEN Aerodrome and proved a great success. The Battalion did very creditably and secured more prizes than any other Infantry Battalion in the Division. The following prizes were obtained:— (1) Two Limbers (4 light draft horses) 1st prize (2) Officers Charger (Style & appearance) (Lieut J.M. Sales - Transport Officer) 2nd prize (3) Blowing Pitcher 3rd prize (4) Water Cart 3rd prize	
Samellies Camp	3rd.		Reinforcements of 5 other ranks joined the Battalion from 36th Divnl Reception Camp. The Battalion with Transport, moved by road to ST MARIE CAPPEL (near CASSEL). Lieut J.R.E. Gemmell was admitted to hospital (sick).	
St. Marie Cappel	4th		The Battalion moved by road to OXELAERE (near Cassel)	
Oxelaere	6th		The Battalion was to move to ST SYLVESTRE CAPPEL, but the order was cancelled on arrival at ST MARIE CAPPEL, and the Battalion returned to its billets at OXELAERE. (Coy D Coy) The Company continued the march to St Sylvester Cappel and billeted there, being billeted independently. The following Officers joined the Battalion. Captain G.A. CHATTERTON. Lieuts W.F. HOGG, M.C. and W.E. GARDINER.	
	7th		The Battalion relieved the 42nd Regiment (French Army) on the night of the	

Army Form C. 2118.

PAGE 2

WAR DIARY
or
INTELLIGENCE SUMMARY.
(Erase heading not required.)

(CONTINUED)

Place	Date	Hour	Summary of Events and Information	Remarks and references to Appendices
LINE	7th July 18		7/8th July in the ST. JANS CAPEL Sector. Bn. H.Q.s were situated in LA MANCHE Char. "A" Coy at VANILLA Farm. "B" & "C" Coys at LA MANCHE Farm and "D" Coy at ST JANS CAPEL. The Commandant of the 42nd Regiment presented the Battn. with a Cow. The Brigade was situated as follows: 1st Battn. in Brigade Reserve, 15th Battn. in the Front Line and the 2nd Battn. in Support. During the period the Battn. was in Brigade Reserve a working party of 2 Officers and 100 other ranks were sent up nightly to the Line.	
-"-	8th		Captain C.H.R. REED M.C. and Captain R.O.H. LAW. M.C. proceeded to England for 6 months tour of duty at home. 15 Other ranks joined the Battn. from 36th Div. Reception Camp.	
MILLAM	10th		Lieut R.A.N. BULLOCH and 14 other ranks joined 36th Divl Reception Camp.	
LINE	12th		2/Lieut. F. LAMONT (18th Dn) joined Battn. 1 Other rank joined from 8th Devons.	
-"-	-"-		Lieut J.C. LEEPER appointed Adjutant vice Lieut (Capt.) G.H.P. WHITFIELD M.C. and to be Acting Captain. 2/Lieut. W.C. WHELAN appointed Assistant Adjutant vice Lieut J.C. LEEPER	

Army Form C. 2118.

PAGE 3

WAR DIARY
INTELLIGENCE SUMMARY.
(Erase heading not required).

Place	Date	Hour	Summary of Events and Information	Remarks and references to Appendices
LINE	July 15/18th		Lieut R.A.N. BULLOCH joined Battalion from 36th Rent. Clapton Camp.	
-"-	15th		The Battn relieved the 15th Battalion in the Right Brigade Sector on the night of 15/16th July. 'A' Coy. Right Front — BENEDICT Farm. 'B' -"- Left -"- — SALVO -"- 'C' -"- Reserve — PUNKAH -"- 'D' -"- Gun too Tank Company. Bn. H.Q's were situated at KOPJE Farm. The 108 Infantry Brigade was on our Left and the 9th Division on our Right 2 Lieut C.R. BEATY was invalided to England (Sick).	
-"-	19th		METEREN was taken by the 9th Division on our right under cover of heavy bombardment. Zero hour 7.55 A.M. Two platoons of "D" Coy. under the command of Lieut J.G. BRANFORD made an unsuccessful raid on the enemy trenches in Co-operation with the Division on our right. "C" & "D" Coys. relieved "A" & "B" Coys. respectively on night of 19/20 Th. 2 Lieut W.E. PARKE and 14 other ranks wounded.	

Army Form C. 2118.

PAGE 4

WAR DIARY or INTELLIGENCE SUMMARY.
(Erase heading not required.)

Place	Date	Hour	Summary of Events and Information	Remarks and references to Appendices
LINE	July 18 19th		No. 5707. Co. M.S. (A/C.S.M.) Leavitt, D.C.M. "D" Coy. went out with a patrol and succeeded in penetrating the enemy wire. At the junction a Machine Gun opened fire and so believed to have killed one (reported wounded & missing). A daylight patrol of "A" Coy under No. 41558 Serjt. T. Arnold succeeded in capturing a prisoner of the ___ Bn whose identification was normal. During the 6 days the Battn. was in the Front Line very active patrolling took place, with a view of obtaining identification, but these patrols met with very little success. The forward companies sent out day as well as night patrols.	
"	20th		3 other ranks killed, 2 died from wounds, 1 wounded & missing (believe killed) and 13 other ranks wounded.	
"	22nd		1 other rank killed, 3 other ranks wounded. Lieut E.D. SCHROEDER joined Battalion from II Corps Temporary Mobile Battn.	
"	23rd		The Bn was relieved on the night of 23/24th. by the 2nd Battn. and on completion of relief moved into Brigade Reserve.	

Army Form C. 2118.

PAGE 5

WAR DIARY or INTELLIGENCE SUMMARY

(Erase heading not required.)

Place	Date	Hour	Summary of Events and Information	Remarks and references to Appendices
LINE	23rd July 16		The Bn. was situated as follows:- Bn. H.Q. at RIFLE RANGE Wood. "A" Coy at ROBERTS Farm. "B" Coy at NOOTE BOONE. "C" Coy at TIBET Farm, and "D" Coy at SENLAC Farm.	
-"-	24th		On the morning of 24th, Bn. H.Q. was heavily shelled by 8 and 12 inch. Captain L.M. BAYLY MC. and 80 other ranks proceeded to BONNINGUES 36th Divisional Training Camp.	
-"-	25th			
-"-	26th		1 other rank killed and 5 other rank wounded. 2 other ranks joined 36th Division Reception Camp (BAVINCHOVE)	
-"-	27/28th		On the night of 27/28th "B" Coy. relieved "A" Coy. (Nucleus Garrison) of BLUE LINE. 1 other rank wounded. During the 8 days the Battn. worked on the BLUE LINE between SCHAEXKEN and FONTAINE HOUCK from 10p to 2am nightly 1 Other rank wounded.	
-"-	30th		27 other ranks joined Battn. from the 36th Division Reception Camp. BONNINGUES.	

WAR DIARY
or
~~INTELLIGENCE SUMMARY~~

Army Form C. 2118.

PAGE 6.

Place	Date	Hour	Summary of Events and Information	Remarks and references to Appendices
LINE	July 16 3/9/16		The Battalion moved into SUPPORT in relief of the 15th Battalion. Bn. H.Q. at LA MANCHE Croix. "B" Coy " LA MANCHE Farm. "D" Coy " FONTAINE HOUCK. "A" Coy at VANILLA Farm. "C" Coy " ROBERTS Farm.	
	"		Major J.A. Mulholland. M.C. proceeded to BONNINGUES to take over command of Battalion School.	
			Honours and Awards.	
			CROIX de GUERRE. No. 8519 C.S.M. Clarke W. D.C.M. " 7265 Sergt. Maguire J.	
			MILITARY MEDAL No. 4115.8 Sergt. Arnold. J.) Awarded Military Medals " 6795 L/Cpl. Stanley. J.a.o.) for gallantry shewn " 9499 " Verner. G.) St. JAN's CAPPEL.	

Stapleton Crawd
Lt. Col. 1st Bn. the Royal Irish Rifles.

WAR DIARY
or
INTELLIGENCE SUMMARY.

Army Form C. 2118.

1 R Irish Rifles

Place	Date	Hour	Summary of Events and Information	Remarks and references to Appendices
In the Field (Suffolk)	1918 Aug 1		The Battalion was in support with Headquarters at La Ibauds Copse Support lines	
	2		8 OR joined Battn from Reception Camp	
	3	Do	Thanksgiving Service at TERDEGHEM	
	4	Do	1 OR to England by Governess. 2 OR wounded (1 at duty)	
	5	Do	1 OR joined Battalion from Reception Camp	
	6	Do	1 OR joined Battn	
	7	Do	2 OR wounded. 1 OR transf. to 2nd Bn. 2nd Lieut E DANIEL and 2nd Lieut J HASLETT joined Battn	
	8	Do	1 OR transf. to 12th Bn. Battn. relieved 15th Bn in the line. A & B Coys Front line. C Coy in Support & D Reserve. Battn. H.Q. in KOPJE FARM	
	9	June	1 OR wounded. 2nd Lieut J Foley joined Reception Camp. Gas projected by L Sperine Co RE on MURAL FARM. A Co Patrol entered farm and found it unoccupied. Capt MC KEARNS struck off strength	
	10	Do	1 OR wounded (at duty)	

WAR DIARY
or
INTELLIGENCE SUMMARY

(Erase heading not required.)

Army Form C. 2118.

PAGE II

Place	Date	Hour	Summary of Events and Information	Remarks and references to Appendices
	1918			
Suis	Aug 11		Inter Company Relief D+C relieved B+A in front line. B moved into reserve and 'A' became Gunto Ostark Co.	
Do	12		1 O.R. wounded. 4 O.R. joined Ruyton Camp	
Do	13		1 O.R. joined Ruyton Camp - Heavy Gas shelling (mustard) round ST JANS CAPPEL and SCHATKEN	
Do	14		4 O.R. wounded (1 gassed) 2nd Lieut P.R.H. MACAULAY wounded on patrol. Rn. W.H. HUTCHISON wounded (gassed)	
Do	15		12 O.R. wounded (11 gassed) 67 O.R. transft from 15th Bn. 98 O.R. Do 12½	
Do	16		12 O.R. gassed - de Gen J.P. HUNT DSO, D.C.M. wounded at PUNKAL FARM on the way to supportem Hd Qrs after which - Major J.A. MULHOLLAND M.C. took over command of the Battn - Captain H. TAYLER 2nd in Command. 1 O.R. to Base underage 2 O.R. joined Ruyton Camp. Battn relieved in line by 15th Bn. and moved into support.	
			'D' VANILLA FARM 'C' HERMITAGE FARM (Nucleus garrison of Blue Line) 'B' ROBERTS FARM 'A' FONTAINE Battn Hd Qrs. LA MANCHE COPSE	
Suffolk	17		3 O.R. wounded	
Do	18			
Do	19			

WAR DIARY or INTELLIGENCE SUMMARY

Army Form C. 2118.
PAGE 111

Place	Date	Hour	Summary of Events and Information	Remarks and references to Appendices
Suffolk	1918 Aug 20		10.R. joined Reninghelst Camp - Battn. area heavily shelled (gas)	
Do	21		2 O.R. Killed 7 O.R. wounded (3 gassed) 1 O.R. taken on strength (Brown Peter) 2 O.R. to Base (underage) 2 O.R. joined Reninghelst Camp. Relieved 2nd Bn in 108th Bde Sector (R. Subsector) 'A' Left front 'B' Right front 'C' Garrison of Blue Line 'D' Nucleus Garrison	
Suffolk	22		14 O.R. wounded (12 gassed)	
Do	23		14 O.R. wounded (5 gassed) 3 O.R. Killed 1 O.R. to England (Contentieux grounds) 3 O.R. joined Reninghelst Camp. Wire cutting shoot - "B" withdrew to Reserve and 'A' took over whole Front Line	
Do	24		1 O.R. Killed 2 O.R. wounded 10 R. jumped to 12th Pm. 9th Bn. Rt. IRISH FUSILIERS about and through the Battn. and gained all objectives - R.I. Fus's held new front line and we remained in old front line & Burmah Suffolk - Line was now S8.c.10.75 - LA BOURSE - SOOT FARM -	

Army Form C. 2118.

WAR DIARY
or
INTELLIGENCE SUMMARY
(Erase heading not required.)

PAGE IV

Place	Date	Hour	Summary of Events and Information	Remarks and references to Appendices
	1918 August (cont'd)		Side of road from S8 c.0.4 - S3 c.7.2 thence along trench E.S3 c.9.5 - S3 d. central - TOMLIN FARM was also captured and took place in advance of the above line. 60 Prisoners and 5 Machine Guns were captured.	
	25		Same. Battn relieved by 9th Rl Innskilling Fusiliers (109th Bde) & moved with 108 Bde into Divisional Reserve. Bn Hd Qrs BOESCHEPE.	
BOESCHEPE	26		Rifleman DUCHART arrested.	
Do	27		Battn moved to ST MARIE CAPPEL.	
ST MARIE CAPPEL	28		Lieut J.S. MACMASTER joined Battalion.	
Do	29		Q.O.R. joined Ruyton Camp.	
Do	30		Lieut CHANDLER H.F. 2nd Lieut TUTTY A.S.B. and WALKER A.W. joined Battalion.	
Do	31		Battalion moved from ST MARIE CAPPEL at 1.30 p.m. to MONT NOIR area. Battn H Qrs BOESCHEPE	

WAR DIARY
or
INTELLIGENCE SUMMARY.

Army Form C. 2118.

Page V

Place	Date	Hour	Summary of Events and Information	Remarks and references to Appendices
	1918 August (cont)		The Divisional Commander visited the Battalion to inspect the Bidouin in the IX Corps Horse Show which assembled at TERDIGHEM today. The Battalion won the first prize for the best Infantry Transport turnout consisting of 1 Cooker, 1 Watercart, 2 Limbers & Park Animals. The Commander Sergeant Clarke was presented with a silver cup and each man drawn with a silver medal.	W Nicholas Lt / Adjt. 1st Regt. Comdg 1st Bn Royal Irish Rifles

107/36

Army Form C. 2118.

1ST. ROYAL IRISH RIFLES

WAR DIARY
or
INTELLIGENCE SUMMARY.
(Erase heading not required.)

PAGE 1

VOL 48

Place	Date	Hour	Summary of Events and Information	Remarks and references to Appendices
MONT NOIR	September 1918			
AREA	1st		The Bn. proceeded to NEUVE EGLISE Area in Divisional Support. Bn.H.Q. at RAG FARM. R.S.M. W. Clarke, (8378) proceeded to the United Kingdom for a 6 months tour of duty.	
(Brethren)				
LINE	3rd		One other ranks wounded.	
(SUPPORT)	4th		Two other ranks killed and 2 other ranks wounded.	
Front LINE	5th/6th MN		The Battalion relieved the 2nd Bn. in the Line. 16 other ranks wounded.	
"	6th		12 other ranks wounded. 2/Lieut. A.S.B. Tutty admitted to hospital N.Y.D.N. 2/Lieut W.A.S. McPherson appointed Acting Captain whilst commanding a company. 30 other ranks joined B.36 Div Reception Camp & photo to Bn.	
"	7th		7 other ranks killed, 28 wounded.	
	8th		The Bn relieved the 24th Bn Royal Welsh Fusiliers (9th ? Bde) in the Line between HYDE PARK Corner and the DOUVE and also Bn	

1st ROYAL IRISH RIFLES WAR DIARY

INTELLIGENCE SUMMARY

Army Form C. 2118.

PAGE 2

Place	Date	Hour	Summary of Events and Information	Remarks and references to Appendices
LINE	September 8th		One platoon of the 2nd Bn R.I. Rifles in Front Line between DOUVE and GOOSEBERRY FARM. 1 other rank killed. 7 wounded. The 15th Bn R.I. Rifles relieved this Bn. in the Line previously held.	
-//-	9th		8 other ranks wounded. 2/Lieut A.M. Bourke, Connaught Rangers, joined Battalion	
-//-	10th		2 other ranks killed, 3 wounded. Lieut Colonel J. Hunt D.S.O. D.C.M. rejoined Bn. from Hospital and took over command.	
-//-	11th		3/Lieut C. Haigh wounded. 3 other ranks killed. 12 wounded. Lieut J.L. Creighton R.I. Fusiliers joined 36 Div Reception Camp and posted to Bn.	
-//-	12th		The Bn. was relieved by the 15th Bn.R.I. Rifles in the HILL 63 Sector, and this Bn (at) relieved the 2nd Bn. R.I. Rifles in the NEUVE EGLISE LINE (Old G.H.Q. Line) Support. 2/Lieut L. Farley Ann. to hospital N.Y.D.N. 5 other ranks wounded.	
SUPPORT.	13th		31 other ranks joined this 36 Div Reception Camp & posted to Bn.	

1ST. ROYAL IRISH RIFLES.

WAR DIARY or INTELLIGENCE SUMMARY.

Army Form C. 2118.

PAGE 3

Place	Date	Hour	Summary of Events and Information	Remarks and references to Appendices
SUPPORT	16th		The Bn. was relieved by the 2nd Bn Royal Irish Fusiliers and proceeded to PIEBROUCK - BERTHEN Training Area. Bn. H.Q. situated in BERTHEN CHATEAU.	
BERTHEN	17th		11 other ranks joined Bn. from Reception Camp.	
-"-	18th		Major J.A. Mulholland M.C. proceeded to the United Kingdom for 6 months tour of duty.	
			16 other ranks joined 36 Div Reception Camp and posted to Bn.	
			75 -"- -"- joined Bn. from Reception Camp.	
-"-	19th		The Bn. moved by road to TERDEGHEM. Transport accompanied Battalion.	
			Lieut W.J. Hogg M.C. appointed Acting Captain (additional)	
TERDEGHEM	20th		The Battalion moved by road to BISSEZEELE. Transport accompanied Battalion.	
BISSEZEELE	23rd		One other rank proceeded to the United Kingdom for temporary commission.	
			5 other ranks joined 36 Div Reception Camp & posted to Bn.	
-"-	24th		Major G.R.H. MAY joined Battalion from the 15th Battn. R.I. Rifles and	

1ST ROYAL IRISH RIFLES.

Army Form C. 2118.

WAR DIARY
or
INTELLIGENCE SUMMARY
(Erase heading not required.)

PAGE 4.

Place	Date	Hour	Summary of Events and Information	Remarks and references to Appendices
BISSEZEELE	September 25th		and took over second in command.	
-,,-	26th		The Battalion moved by road to TUNNELLING CAMP (near PROVEN) accompanied by Bn Transport.	
TUNNELLING CAMP	27th		The Battalion moved by road to P.Camp (on the POPERINGHE – WOESTEN Road) Transport accompanied Battn.	
-,,-			11 other ranks joined 36 Div Reception Camp & rostd to Bn.	
"P" CAMP	28th		The Bn moved by rail to the WHITE CHATEAU area, EAST of YPRES on the YPRES-MENIN Road. Bn transport moved by road.	
YPRES WHITE CHATEAU	29th		The Bn moved by road to WESTHOEK to Divisional Support & occupied "PILL" Boxes in this area. Lieut J.L. Creighton R.I. Fusiliers Junior Bn and appointee Battn Burial Officer.	
WESTHOEK	30th	6.A.M.	The Bn moved to BECELAERE area (NORTH) still in Divisional Support, and at 4.30 p.m. the same day moved to a position 600+ E. of TERHAND. Bn H.Q. in a "PILL BOX." Coys & Bn HQ personnel took up positions along ridge in support of 2nd Bn.	

WAR DIARY
INTELLIGENCE SUMMARY

1/Royal Irish Rifles

Army Form C. 2118.

PAGE 5

Place	Date	Hour	Summary of Events and Information	Remarks and references to Appendices
	30th		**HONOURS and AWARDS.** The following decorations were awarded to Officers, NCO's and Riflemen during the month:-	
			MILITARY CROSS	
			2/Lieut. (A/Capt.) W.A.S. McPherson.	
			" J. Hazlett.	
			D.C.M.	
			No 16549 L/c. R. Herdman.	
			MILITARY MEDALS	
			No 40615 L/c. W. Yardley	
			" 41678 Rfn. W. Woodruff.	
			" 43918 Sgt. J. Robertson.	
			" 9876 " C. Lawrence.	
			" 12211 L/c. J. Montgomery	

In the field
10th October 1918

W Ancketell Lieut A/Adjutant
1st Bn. The Royal Irish Rifles

1st Bn. The Royal Irish Rifles.

WAR DIARY
or
INTELLIGENCE SUMMARY
(Erase heading not required.)

Army Form C. 2118.

Vol 49
PAGE 1

Place	Date	Hour	Summary of Events and Information	Remarks and references to Appendices
	October 1918			
IN SUPPORT	1st.		The Bn moved up from SUPPORT to take over the LINE South of DADIZEELE from the 2nd Bn. & was relieved by the 15th Bn. Bn H.Q. was situated in "PILL BOX" CAVANDER HOUSE Casualties:- 5 other ranks killed, 39 other ranks wounded. 2/Lieut. A.S.D. Jetty to England (sick) 29.9.18. 2/Lieut. H.F. Chandler to England (sick) 29.9.18. 11 other ranks joined from Gnrl Reception Camp & posted to Bn.	
IN LINE	2nd		A minor operation was carried out by the Bn. (supported by the 15th Bn). The operation succeeded on the left flank and failed on right flank owing to intense machine gun fire. The following places were attacked:- DIBSLAND and SOMERBY farm attacked by "B" Coy with "C" Coy in Support (LEFT FLANK) and CLARA BOROUGH House attacked by "D" Coy supported by "A" Coy. (RIGHT FLANK). The left flank withdrew to old position owing to right flank not being haven reached objective. Casualties. Officers killed. 2/Lieut J.C. Haigh (R.D. Ins attc) Other ranks killed 13. Wounded 2/Lieut W.C. Gardiner, & Capt. H. Taylor. Wounded 59. " A.W. Walker " A.A.F. McManus Missing 28. 2 " Wounded 1 " A.W.M. 1 " Missing 1 " Died from wounds Lieut. R. Murphy.	

WAR DIARY or INTELLIGENCE SUMMARY

Army Form C. 2118.
PAGE 2.

(Erase heading not required.)

Place	Date	Hour	Summary of Events and Information	Remarks and references to Appendices
	October '18.			
IN LINE	2nd.		Casualties:- 2 other ranks wounded. Lieut. A.H. Nicholson & Lieut. J.A. Maxwell joined Bn. from Divs Reception Camp.	
— " —	4th.	6 a.m.	One platoon of "A" Coy under 2nd Lieut. J. Lamont, made an unsuccessful local attack on two "Pill boxes" at K 30 c. 1. 5. (Ref Maps 28 N.W. + 28 N.E. DADIZEELE Sheet 29.) which was strongly held by the enemy with machine guns. Enemy counter-attacked but was repulsed. The Bn. was relieved by the 15th. Bn. and proceeded to positions in TERHAND area. The captures between the 1st and the 4th. inst. 4 (heavy) M. Guns, 1 (light) M. Guns and 1 Anti tank Gun. Casualties 6 other ranks killed. 15 wounded, and 6 missing. Captain H. Taylor transferred to England wounded. 16 other ranks joined Bn. as reinforcements from D.R. Camp.	
	11 - " -		D.R. Camp + hostes to Bn. 4 O.R. joined B.R.C. + hostes to Bn.	
TERHAND	5th		3 other ranks wounded. Lieut R.A.N. Bullock and Lieut L. Farley to England (sick).	

WAR DIARY
or
INTELLIGENCE SUMMARY.

Army Form C. 2118.

PAGE 3

Place	Date	Hour	Summary of Events and Information	Remarks and references to Appendices
	October 18.			
TERHAND	11th.		The Bn. moved to REUTEL Area (near BECELAERE) and carried out re-organisation of Companies &c.	
		2 p.m.	A.M. Bondo (Connaught Rangers attached) wounded himself accidentally.	
---"---	13th.	19.15	The Bn. moved to assembly positions at WORTHINGTON FARM (Map DADIZEELE Sheet 29) in support of 15th Bn. as follows:—	
			"D" Coy. LEFT front and "A" Coy LEFT Support	
			"B" " RIGHT " " " "	
			"B" " RIGHT " —"—	
			Bn. H.Q. were established at MAIL HOUSE	
SUPPORT	14th		The Bn. passed through the 15th Bn., E. of MOORSEELE and attacked GULLEGHEM without Artillery support, and was held up by 3 belts of barbed wire and heavy machine gun opposition about 500* W of GULLEGHEM.	
LINE		11.00	Bn. again attacked GULLEGHEM attempting an outflanking movement but only progressed about 200*. With rifle fire we brought down a german reconnaissance machine and captured the Aviators. (One Officer and One N.C.O.)	

WAR DIARY

INTELLIGENCE SUMMARY

Army Form C. 2118.

PAGE 4

Place	Date	Hour	Summary of Events and Information	Remarks and references to Appendices
	October '18			
LINE	14th		Casualties:- Officers wounded:- Captain & Adjutant J.C. Taylor. Other ranks:-	
			Lieut A.H. Nicholson. Killed 23	
			2 Lieut A.M. Jeffares. Wounded 92	
			Missing 8	
			Died from wounds 1	
			22 other ranks Joined Battalion from D.R. Camp	
			3 " " " " " " D.R.C	
			2 " " " " " " D.R.C	
LINE	15th		The Battalion again attacked (with Artillery barrage) GULLEGHEM and reached objective 1000ᵗ E of GULLEGHEM where the 2nd Bn. passed through our Bn. and reached line of Corps objective (HEULE). A gap occurred between our Bn. on the night and of the Division on the left and was filled up by our Battalion thus swinging to its to the front line again. Casualties:- Officers wounded o/Captain W.T. Hogg M.C. Other ranks killed 3	
			2 Lieut J.A. Maxwell " " wounded 24	
			" G. Branford " " missing 1	
			" Killed Lieut E.J. Williams	

WAR DIARY
INTELLIGENCE SUMMARY
(Erase heading not required.)

Army Form C. 2118.
PAGE 5

Place	Date	Hour	Summary of Events and Information	Remarks and references to Appendices
LINE	October 15th		2/Lieut. W.C. Whelan took over the duties of Acting Adjutant vice Captain & Adjutant J.C. Leeper wounded, and Lieut. W.C. Gardiner to over the duties of Asst. Adjutant	
LINE	16th		The Battn. was relieved, by the 9th Division on the night and 2nd Bn. R.I. Rifles on the left, and moved into Billets at ROLLINGHEMCAPPEL where the Bn. Transport & Engineer Battalion. Casualties. - 3 other ranks wounded. Bn. captured between the 14th & 16th One Howitzer.	
ROLLINGHEMCAPPEL	18th		The Battalion, accompanied by transport, marched to LENDELEDE to new billets. 3 other ranks joined from D.R.C. & posted to Bn.	
LENDELEDE	19th	4.30	The 13 Bn. moved to assembly positions 1000* E. of HULSTE & Liliotte for the night. (107 Bn. in support of 109 (Bde). One thousand wounded.	
SUPPORT	20th	02.00	Commenced crossing the RIVER LYS and formed up on BEVEREN - DESSENGHEM road. Advanced in support of 15th Bn. up to 17.00 who reached a line 500* S.E. of DEERLYCK - WAEREGHEM road and 1st Bn. went through the 15th Bn. and reached GAVERBEK (stream) during night.	

WAR DIARY
or
INTELLIGENCE SUMMARY

(Erase heading not required.)

Army Form C. 2118.
PAGE 6

Place	Date	Hour	Summary of Events and Information	Remarks and references to Appendices
LINE	October /18			
	20th		Captured by Bn:- 1, 6" naval gun - Daimler tractor.	
			Casualties:- Officers wounded. Lieut. W.J. Linton & Rev. W.H. Hutcheson Army Chaplain.	
			Other ranks " 21. Missing 1.	
"—	21st.		The Battalion continued the Advance in a South-easterly direction and reached the line KNOCK (N.W.) to the GAVERBEK (Stream) and dug in and held the position occupied.	
			Casualties:- Officers killed - Lieut. E. Daniels. Other ranks killed 4.	
			" wounded - Lieut. J. Gardiner. " — wounded 13.	
			" " - Captain L.M. Bayly. M.C. " — Missing 1.	
			5 other ranks joined Bn. from Divisional Reception Camp. &	
			Captain O.W. Keating joined D.R.C. & posted to Battn.	
			The Bn continued to hold the line occupied.	
"—	22nd		Casualties:- Captain L.M. Bayly M.C. Died from wounds in C.C.S.	
			" J.R. Cannon Rame (attached) wounded	
			Other ranks wounded - 9 Missing 1.	
			2 other ranks joined D.R. Camp & posted to Bn.	

WAR DIARY
or
INTELLIGENCE SUMMARY

Army Form C. 2118.

PAGE 7

Place	Date	Hour	Summary of Events and Information	Remarks and references to Appendices
LINE	October 15	22nd	Congratulations received from MARSHAL FOCH, Commanding Allied Forces, and the Divisional Commander, Major General C. Coffin V.C. D.S.O. on the splendid work done by the 36th Division in operations since 14th October 1918 (Copy attached).	
	23rd		The Bn. continued advancing, passing through the 2nd Bn. on KLIJTBERG Ridge and advanced as far as HULSBOSCH Ridge & dug in and held the line until relieved by the 109 Inf Bde., and then moved into Billets at DESSELGHEM on night 23rd/24th., where the Bn. transport rejoined. Casualties - Officers wounded - Lieut. F. Lamont. Other ranks wounded 6. Congratulations and thanks received from the II Corps Commander, Lieut. General C.N. Jacob, on the Splendid work done by the 36th Division. (Copy attached)	
DESSELGHEM	24th		Captain & Adjutant J.C. Leeper rejoined Bn. from hospital (wounded) & resumed the duties of Adjutant & Lieut W.C. Whelan resumed duties of Asst. Adjutant.	

Army Form C. 2118.

WAR DIARY
~~INTELLIGENCE~~ SUMMARY
(Erase heading not required.)

PAGE 8.

Instructions regarding War Diaries and Intelligence Summaries are contained in F. S. Regs., Part II. and the Staff Manual respectively. Title pages will be prepared in manuscript.

Place	Date	Hour	Summary of Events and Information	Remarks and references to Appendices
DESSELGHEM	October 18 26th		The Battalion marched to LENDELEDE accompanied by Bn. Transport. Congratulations received from Divisional Commander, Major General C Coffin V.C. D.S.O. on the Splendid way in which the Division fought on 25th October '18. (Copy attached).	
LENDELEDE	27th		The Battalion marched to the BELLEGHEM Area (South of COURTRAI) accompanied by Bn. Transport. 3 other ranks joined D.R. Camp & poster to Bn.	
BELLEGHEM	29th		Revd W.A. Hutcheson, newly Chaplain, rejoined (one from Hospital (wounded). Captain E.J. Hoare joined Battalion from 36th Div Reception Camp. 2nd Lieut R.D. Eastly + J.S. Aspell and 60 other ranks joined Bn. from D.R.C. The following decorations were awarded to Officers, N.C.O's and Riflemen during the month:—	
— " —	30th			
— " —	31st		HONOURS and AWARDS.	

MILITARY CROSS.
a/Captain C.J. Cullen (R.D. for attm.)

MILITARY MEDALS
10756 Corpl. A. Catalani.
9876 Rfmn W.S. McBratney
16231 —   J. Bailey
40855 L.Cpl W. Baxter.

(signed) Lieut Col
Commanding 12th Bn
October /31/18

Copy

> ORDERLY ROOM
> No.
> DATE
> 1st BN. R. IR. RIFLES

22/10/18.

36th Division.

Marshal FOCH visited the Army Commander to-day and asked him to send his congratulations to the II Corps and to the 9th, 29th and 36th Divisions for their splendid work in the operations since the 14th October. Please communicate the above to all ranks.

To all Divisional Units.

The Divisional Commander congratulates all ranks on the splendid fighting qualities exhibited by them which have won this approbation from Marshal FOCH.

(Sgd.) A. G. THOMSON,
Lieut. Colonel, G.S.
36th (ULSTER) Division.

22nd October 1918.

Copy   36th Division G.T. 382

All Divisional Units.

       The army Commander has sent a message through the Corps Commander to all ranks of the 36th Division expressing his satisfaction with the way the Division fought on 25.10.18.

       In transmitting this message I congratulate the Division on the way they fought yesterday, attacking a strong position held by a force numerically greater than the attackers, and by their bearing earning the message of approval from the Army Commander.

                                    (Sgd.) C. COFFIN,

                                                           Major-General
                            Commanding 36th (ULSTER) Division.

26th October 1918.

WAR DIARY

H.Q., II Corps,
22nd Oct., 1918.

Major-General C. Coffin, V.C., D.S.O.,
Commanding 36th Division.

=================================

The 36th (Ulster) Division has been fighting continuously since the 28th Septr. in the operations in FLANDERS. The spirit, dash and initiative shewn by all ranks have been splendid and beyond all praise. The leadership displayed by yourself and your Brigade and other Commanders could not have been better. The conditions under which the men have had to fight have been and are still very trying, but nothing seems to stop your gallant Division.

I have also been much struck with the good Staff work of the Division and it is very creditable to all concerned.

Will you kindly express to the Commanders, Staffs and all ranks of the Division my heartiest congratulations and thanks for their work.

When the history is written of what the Division has done in FLANDERS during the past month, it will prove to be a record of magnificent fighting and wonderful progress, for during this period an advance has been made of about 25 miles over the worst of country and under the heaviest machine gun fire ever experienced in this war. This advance has entailed constant fighting but the 36th Division has overcome every obstacle and has proved itself one of the best fighting divisions in the Army, well commanded and well staffed.

My best wishes to you all.

(Sgd.) C.N. JACOB,
Lieutenant-General,
Commanding II Corps.

To all Divisional Units.

=================================

In forwarding the above laudatory remarks of the Corps Commander, the Divisional Commander again wishes to congratulate all ranks of the Division on the magnificent way in which they have fought and worked.

Lieut. Colonel, G.S.,
36th (Ulster) Division.

23/10/18.

ORDERLY ROOM
1st BN. R. IR. RIFLES.

Army Form C. 2118.

PAGE 1

WAR DIARY
or
INTELLIGENCE SUMMARY
(Erase heading not required.)

Instructions regarding War Diaries and Intelligence Summaries are contained in F. S. Regs., Part II. and the Staff Manual respectively. Title Pages will be prepared in manuscript.

Remarks and references to Appendices

1ST. BN. THE ROYAL IRISH RIFLES.

Place	Date	Hour	Summary of Events and Information	Remarks
	1918 NOVEMBER			
BELLEGHEM	1st	5 pm	The Battalion moved by route to RECKEM Area accompanied by the Bn Transport. Captain E.J. Hoare, 2/Lieuts. J.S. Aspin, and W.P.D. Cutley joined Bn (30.10.18) from the Divisional Reception Camp. 34 other ranks joined the Battn. from the 36 D.R. Camp.	
RECKEM Area	3rd	9 am	The Bn. proceeded to MOUSCRON by route march with Bn Transport. 2/Lieut. W.J.L. Lloyd Jones Bn from the 36th D.R. Camp. — 2/Lieut. J.L. Creighton, R.S. Fables invalides to England (sick).	
MOUSCRON	4th		4 other ranks joined D.R.C. and posted to the Bn.	
"	5th		The Bn Sports Meeting took place and was a great success. (Programme of events attached)	

2449 Wt. W14957/M90 759,000 1/16 J.B.C. & A. Forms/C.2118/12.

Army Form C. 2118.

PAGE 2.

WAR DIARY
or
INTELLIGENCE SUMMARY
(Erase heading not required.)

Place	Date	Hour	Summary of Events and Information	Remarks and references to Appendices
MOUSCRON	Nov. 1918. 7th.		The Bn. took part in the 107th Inf. Brigade Sports meeting which were also a great success. (Programme of Sports attached)	
-"-	8th.		No. 7095 C.S.M. W. Sumner, D.C.M., M.M. rejoins the Bn. from the 1st Bn R.I. Fusiliers	
-"-	10th.	23.00	The Official news of the signing of the ARMISTICE by Germany received. The Buglers of the Battalion sounded the CEASE FIRE. 15 other ranks joined the Bn. from the D.R. Camp.	
-"-	15th.		Lieut. W. Miller joined the Bn. from the D.R. Camp.	
-"-	16th.		Lieuts. D. Black, M.M., J.R. Edwards, M.M., & J. Connolly, 3/R.I. Fus. James Bn. from the 36 D.R. Camp.	
-"-	17th.		Lieut. J.C. Grummell, M.M., and 4 other ranks joined Bn. from D.R. Camp.	
-"-	22nd.		16 other ranks joined Bn. from the 36 D.R. Camp.	

Army Form C. 2118.

WAR DIARY
or
INTELLIGENCE SUMMARY
(Erase heading not required.)

PAGE 3

Place	Date	Hour	Summary of Events and Information	Remarks and references to Appendices
MOUSCRON	Nov. '18			
	25th		The undermentioned Officers and 21 other ranks joined the Bn. from the 36 D.R. Camp:—	
			2/Lieut. J. Miller 3/R. IR. FUS. 2/Lieut. C. Franklin. 31/Lancs. Regt.	
			—„— J. J. Reid —„— E.A. Rathbone. 51st (Grad) D. L. I.	
			—„— S. Stanfield —„— C.S. Saunsbury. Essex Regt.	
			—„— J. Smith	
	26th		2/Lieut. J. G. Stokes and Lieut. J.R. Mills R.I. Fusiliers joined Bn. from 36 Div. Reptn Camp.	
			HONOURS and AWARDS.	
			The following decorations were awarded to Officers, Non-commissioned Officers and Riflemen during the month:—	

The
    Officer Commanding
        1st Bn The Royal Irish Rifles.

    I enclose herewith Christmas greeting from General Sir. H.H.
Wislon. K.C.B., D.S.O. Colonel of the Regiment.

Belfast
23.12.18.

                                                    Lieut Colonel
                      Commanding Depot The Royal Irish Rifles.

DEPOT
23 DEC. 1918
THE ROYAL IRISH RIFLES

WAR DIARY
or
INTELLIGENCE SUMMARY

Army Form C. 2118.

PAGE 4.

Place	Date	Hour	Summary of Events and Information	Remarks and references to Appendices
MOUSCRON.	Nov. 7/8		1) **Distinguished Service Order.** Major. E. A. F. May. 2) **Military Crosses.** Captain H. Taylor. " W.R. Bell. 2/Lieut J. McKenna (Attd 147 T.M. Batty) " F. Lamont. " A. McIntosh. " W.J. Lenton Rev. W.H. Hutchison. C.F. 3) **Distinguished Conduct Medals** 40615 L/Cpl. W. Yardley. M.M. 47277 Rfn D. Bow. 18593 C.S.M. J.J. Mackey. 4) <u>La Medaille D'Honneur Avec Glaives en Vermeil</u>	5) **Military Medals** No 8719 C.S.M. J. Greene. 14319 Sergt. W. Gourley. 103 " J. Lanigan. 8193 Cpl. J. Willott. 79 L/C. W. Barkhead. 85 " J. Ferguson 18800 " J.A. Smith 6177 Cpl. J. Leathem 30229 Rfn W. Savage 40926 " J.D. Wilson. 47307 " W. House. 3260 " W. Humphreys. 22754 " E Cole. 40644 " A. Brown. 44009 " W. Seibert. 13817 " J. Warnock. 6) **Bar to Military Medals.** No 10736 Cpl. A. Carolan M.M. " 9098 " W.A. Woods. M.M.	

Army Form C. 2118.

WAR DIARY
or
INTELLIGENCE SUMMARY.
(Erase heading not required.)

WR 51 PAGE 1

Place	Date	Hour	Summary of Events and Information	Remarks and references to Appendices
	DEC '18.		1ST. BN. THE ROYAL IRISH RIFLES.	
MOUSCRON	7th		Captain E.C. ROBB joined the Battalion from the 36 Div. Reception Camp.	
	8th		70 other ranks joined the Bn from the Reception Camp.	
	25th	13.00	Christmas Day was celebrated by the Bn. being a Christmas Dinner, which was thoroughly enjoyed by all ranks. The Brigade Commander visited the Dinner of the N.C.O.s and Riflemen and wished them all a Happy Christmas	
		19.30	The Officers of the Bn held their Christmas Dinner in the Convent Mouscron. Christmas Greetings were received from Gen. Sir H.H. Wilson, Colonel of the Royal Irish Rifles (Gy attached)., G.O.C. 5th Army., G.O.C. 36th Division., G.O.C. 107 Inf Bde., and 3rd (Res) Bn. R.I. Rifles, Larkebury Plain., Lieut J.L. DORSEY, Medical Corps, U.S.A. Joined Bn. (omitted from last months Diary).	

HONOURS and AWARDS.

The undermentioned Officers, Warrant Officer, N.C.O.'s & Riflemen have been awarded

19.11.18

Army Form C. 2118.

PAGE 2

WAR DIARY
or
INTELLIGENCE SUMMARY.
(Erase heading not required.)

Place	Date	Hour	Summary of Events and Information	Remarks and references to Appendices
NOUS CRON.	Dec '18		Decorations for service in the Field as follows during the month:—	
			(a) French Croix De Guerre a l'Ordre Division (Silver Star)	
			No. 9280 C.Q.M.S. W. McFaull.	
			(b) French Croix De Guerre a l'Ordre Regiment (Bronze Star)	
			Lieut. J. M. Tate.	
			No. 7146 R.Q.M.S. L.C. Corrigan.	
			8875 Lce. Cpl. J. Stevenson.	
			14927 Sergt. J. Stooks (attd. 107 Inf. Bde.).	
			No. 103 Sergt. J. Langan.	
			" 43917 Lce. Cpl. A. J. Ludlow.	
			(c) Mentioned in Despatches	
			Captain G. W. Edwards.	
			" J. C. Leper.	
			(d) Divisional Complimentary Cards.	

(OVER)

WAR DIARY
or
INTELLIGENCE SUMMARY.
(Erase heading not required.)

Army Form C. 2118.

PAGE 3.

Place	Date	Hour	Summary of Events and Information	Remarks and references to Appendices
MOUSCRON	Dec. '18.		Divisional Complimentary Card. (Cnts).	

Nº 9933 ¾C.Q.M.S. Clover J.
" 41614 Sergt. Cole E.
" 10569 Cpl. Proctor H.
" 46851 " Jarvis W.
" 20393 L/c. Curran B.
" 40879 Rfn. Jackson W.
" 9370 " Cully M.
" 500 " Lomax R.
" 588 " Kinkaid J.
" 1115 " Brown J.
" 44040 " Vincent W.
" 9218 " Jackson B.

Nº 9562 Sgt. Hemisher C.
" 2125 " Taylor L.
" 10588 Cpl. Patterson J.
" 49168 " Chambers J.
" 115 L/c. Campbell J.
" 1356 Rfn. Wilson J.
" 50348 " Patterson J.
" 44365 " Ray A.
" 119 " Coates S.
" 1316 " Black J.
" 9151 Rfn. Dixon F.Q.
" 3966 Rfn. Grant R.

Nº 8778 Sgt. O Donnelly.
" 47315 Cpl. M. Kill.
" 16992 " R. Beatie.
" 16184 " A. Bell.
" 21160 L/c. W. Hall.
" 42929 Rfn. J. Brown.
" 9280 " J. Mc Kay.
" 44639 " C. Clayson.
" 45523 " H. Mc Sharee.
" 18100 " D. Linton.
" 6884 L/c. J. Campbell.
" 5671 Rfn. M. Allen.

1/1/19

Clarke, Captain.
Adjutant 1st Bn. The Royal Irish Rifles.

Army Form C. 2118.

WAR DIARY
or
INTELLIGENCE SUMMARY.
(Erase heading not required.)

FIRST BATTN. THE ROYAL IRISH RIFLES.

Place	Date	Hour	Summary of Events and Information	Remarks and references to Appendices
	Jan'y 1919.			
MOUSCRON.	1st.		2 other ranks proceeded to Concentration Camp for Demobilisation. 5 other ranks joined 36 D.R.C. and posted to the Battalion.	
-"-	2nd		Q.M.S.J. Murray D.C.M. proceeded to United Kingdom and 6 other ranks. (Regular Leave).	
-"-	6th		1 other rank proceeded to United Kingdom (Regular Leave) and 1 to Concentration Camp.	
-"-	7th		2 other ranks proceeded to United Kingdom " "	
-"-	8th		2 other ranks proceeded to United Kingdom " "	
-"-	9th		Captain J.W. Foley joined Battalion.	
-"-	11th		3 other ranks proceeded to United Kingdom (Regular Leave), and 9 O.R. to Concentration Camp for Demobilisation	
-"-	12th		12 other ranks to Concentration Camp for Demobilisation	
-"-	13th		9 other ranks to -"- -"- -"-	
-"-	19th		Lieut. R.E. McGuire and 1 other rank to Disposal Station for Demobilisation. 5 other ranks joined 36 D.R. Camp & posted to Battn.	
-"-	20th		2/Lt. T.H. Arthurs 51st (Grad) D.L.I. to Disposal Station for Demobilisation.	

P.T.O.

Army Form C. 2118.

WAR DIARY
or
INTELLIGENCE SUMMARY
(Erase heading not required.)

PAGE 2.

Place	Date	Hour	Summary of Events and Information	Remarks and references to Appendices
	JAN '19.			
MOUSCRON.	21st		Lieut J. Smith R.I.Fus. and 4 other ranks to Disposal Station for Demobilisation.	
"	22nd		" 2/Lt Carr R.I.Fus and 5 " " " " " "	
"	25th		3 other ranks to Disposal Station for Demobilisation.	
"	26th		25 " " " to Disposal Station " - " -	
"	27th		9 " " " " " "	
"	29th		5 " " " to Disposal Station for Demobilisation.	
"	31st		" " " to Disposal Station for Demobilisation.	
			The following Officers and other ranks have been awarded the decorations as under during the month:-	
			Belgian Croix de Guerre.	
			Captain Q.M. G.W. Edwards.	
			" & Adjt. J.C. Keeper.	
			No 5399 Sgt. J. McDonnell	
			" 4065 Cpl. Ins. Gardiner R.C.m. M.M.	
			" 16549 " R. Gardiner D.C.M.	
			" 47469 T/C J. Carter D.C.M.	
			D.C. Medal. Meritorious Service Medal.	
			No 7750 C.S.m. J. Murray No 9364 Sgt. W. Clarke.	

31/1/19.

J. Keeper Captain
Adjutant 1st Bn. The Royal Irish Rifles.

WAR DIARY
or
INTELLIGENCE SUMMARY.

Army Form C. 2118.

Vol 53

1st Battn The Royal Irish Rifles

Place	Date	Hour	Summary of Events and Information	Remarks and references to Appendices
MUSCRON	February 1/19		The C.O. Major Goodwin visited the Bn and was introduced to all officers present.	
"	2nd		The C.O. proceeded to join the 7th Royal Berkshires	
"	4		Capt H.C. McD. Steadman M.C. relinquished the acting	
"	5		Rank of Capt. he had assumed 9 Dec 1918	
"			2nd Lieut D. M. Gillespie was attached to the Bn for service	
"			and proceeded with 2 pl to 4 A Coy from Kibo	
"	6		Capt H. Folus & Capt E. Shore proceeded to France to	
"			proceeding orders but on arrival there at Liège	
"			the C.O. were that Majors of the Royal Irish Rif.	

WAR DIARY
or
INTELLIGENCE SUMMARY.
(Erase heading not required.)

Army Form C. 2118.
SHEET No 2

Place	Date	Hour	Summary of Events and Information	Remarks and references to Appendices
MUSCRON	8		2/Lt Stoke proceeded to UK prior to proceeding forward with R.A.F. Horse Transport Repair Depot	
"			Lieut J E O'Sullivan taken over the duties of Transport Officer Capt Cash having proceeded on to attend an advanced course at Cambridge	
"	10		2/Lt Whitton took over the duties of Acting Adjutant vice Capt Shepard to [?].	
			2/Lt E Emmett proceeded to UK prior to proceeding to [?] [?] and 2/Lt [?] his Rifles	
			Capt (Rev) W Patterson MC [?] 2nd Bn [?] Lancers appointed Educational Officer to the Bn. C.S.M. Mackay appointed Educational N.C.O.	
			Lieut W E Hazard appointed Demobilization Officer vice [?]	
			W/Ed from 10.12.18	
	11		Lieut O.H. proceeded to proposal School of Demobilization. H. W Miller proceeded to UK from proceeding to Sch 2 at Royal Institute	

P.T.O.

Army Form C. 2118.

PAGE 3

WAR DIARY
or
INTELLIGENCE SUMMARY.
(Erase heading not required.)

Instructions regarding War Diaries and Intelligence Summaries are contained in F. S. Regs., Part II. and the Staff Manual respectively. Title pages will be prepared in manuscript.

Place	Date	Hour	Summary of Events and Information	Remarks and references to Appendices
MUSCRON	11		O.R. proceeded to Concentration Camp prior to demobilisation	
"	13		O.R. proceeded to Concentration Camp prior to demobilisation	
"	14		Capt. P.W. Keating proceeded to U.K. prior to proceeding overseas with 2nd B.E.F. on special duty	
"			1 Other Rank killed	
"	15		16 O.R. proceeded to Concentration Camp for demobilisation	
"			The General Officer arrived with Bath. rolls dated 7th Feb'y & Saturday 8th Feb'y. O/R on 8th Feb'y hours numbering 29 boys. He started & on one day one rest in the journey	
"			No. B.n and one rest in the journey	
"			10 O.R. proceeded to Concentration Camp prior to demobilisation.	
"	17		No. 43893 Sergeant T. [?] M.M. was awarded the Military Medal	
"			2 O.R. wounded arrived at Donoured Beeston Camps and taken by Sh. L.	
"			1 1/6 Welsh here a day to U.K. prior to proceeding overseas with the 2nd B.E.F.	
"			Royal 91st Regiment to be known under gate at Platoons 3 to 6 inclusive	
"	18		3 O.R. joined Battn. from the Base	
"	19		Major F.W.Marsh received a Brigade Sub Office on leave to U.K.	
"			Orders for demob'n of Bat. recvd	
"	20		14 O.R. proceeded to Concentration Camp prior to demobilisation	
"	21		15 O.R. proceeded to Concentration Camp prior to demobilisation	

P.T.O.

WAR DIARY or INTELLIGENCE SUMMARY

Army Form C. 2118. PAGE 4.

Place	Date	Hour	Summary of Events and Information	Remarks and references to Appendices
MUSCRON	Feb 1919 22		Bn. Lt. Col. and Capt. W.R.B.W.H.C. instructed to duty with Re.	
	"		12th Royal Fusiliers and district of strength of B?	
	"		Coll. Officer + two O.R.s earlier, will also to 12th Royal not Rifles + check off the march of the Bn. absolut. P.S.G. Fennell + 2/Lt. Millar	
	23		2 O.R.s and 3 mules to dismounter. 1 O.R. sample tick sick.	
	24		45 O.R.s acceded to Concentration Camp No 11 proceeding to dismobilisation 155 O.R.s were transferred to 13th Royal Irish Rifle to form Army of Austria Rhine. Strength reduced to 4 Offrs + 137th Royal Irish Rifles + 1 Royal (Army 150 5th Offrs attached the new base leaving 4 O.R.s. 107 L.M.B.	
			8 O.R.s. 107 L.M.B. were transferred to 12th Royal Irish Rifles + 1 Roy. Offrs strength of Bn.	
	25		Orders received for Battn to be reduced to Cadre strength. Lieut. Whelan, Lieut. Connolly and 2 O.R.s Black were transferred to 12th Bn. Royal Irish Rifles and were struck off the strength of the Bn.	
			1 O.R. taken on strength from 107 L.M.B.	
	26		42 O.R.s were transferred to 12th Reg. as not killed.	
	27		16 O.R.s transferred from 12th 13th Royal Irish Rifles to this Unit.	
	28		10 O.R.s proceeded on transfer to 12th Royal Irish Rifles.	

WAR DIARY

PAGE 5 Army Form C. 2118.

Place	Date	Hour	Summary of Events and Information	Remarks and references to Appendices
MUSCRON	February 25 1919		Major M. Affleck, M.C. & Lieut. 6 K. McCauley joined the Bn. from 15.22 Irish Riflers.	
	28.2.19		A.G. Garnett S/Lieut ? B. The Royal Irish Riflers.	

Army Form C. 2118.

WAR DIARY
or
INTELLIGENCE SUMMARY
(Erase heading not required.)

Instructions regarding War Diaries and Intelligence Summaries are contained in F.S. Regs., Part II. and the Staff Manual respectively. Title Pages will be prepared in manuscript.

1st. Battn. The Royal Irish Rifles.

Vol 54

Place	Date	Hour	Summary of Events and Information	Remarks and references to Appendices
MUSCRON	March 1919			
	1		20 O.R. demobilized.	
	3		O.R. joined Bn. from S. Irish Band.	
			21 O.R. ¾ to Calais & Wareham Concentration Camps.	
			6 O.R. proceed to Concentration Camp Lille prior to demobilization.	
	4		3 O.R. proceed to Concentration Camp. 36 O.R. changes to 12th Rifles.	
			Lieut. A Coey struck off strength being demobilized on leave.	
			20 O.R. posted to 5th Bn. R. Ir. Rif.	
	5		3 O.R. posted to 12th Bn Royal Irish Rifles.	
	6		Capt. P. Mullins struck off strength on being appointed C.O.	
	7		G.H.Q. No. 855 Area Employment Co Calais.	
			2 O.R. transferred to 12th Bn Royal Irish Rifles.	
	10		1 O.R. transferred to 12th Bn Royal Irish Rifles.	
			15 O.R. proceed to Concentration Camp Lille prior to demobilization.	
	11		1 O.R. joined Bn. from Infantry Base Depot Havre.	

2449 Wt. W14957/M90 750,000 1/16 J.B.C. & A. Forms/C.2118/12.

WAR DIARY or INTELLIGENCE SUMMARY

Army Form C. 2118. Sheet 2

Place	Date	Hour	Summary of Events and Information	Remarks and references to Appendices
MUSCRON	11		1st R transferred to 12th B. Royal Scots R.C. 2nd R. proceeded to concentration camp for demobilisation 10th R transferred to England that strict off strength. Appointment sanctioned appointment of Lt Col C Gardner as adjutant (acty capt) privileged 17.2.19 vice Capt.	
	15		Capt. H. Pegler to England on course 2.2.19	
	17		Rev Capt. G. Swan R.C. Chaplain attached to Unit.	
	18		3rd R transferred to 12th B. Royal Scots R.C. Capt. V Dorsey M.E. M.O.A. proceed to SMO 2nd Army. Lt. J. R. Mills proceed to concentration camp file no. 6 for demobilisation.	
	22		Capt. V. M. Ames transferred to 12th B. Royal Scots Rifles Capt. W. C. Gardner attached to 12th B. R. Scots from R. Scots Rifles. 12th R proceed to concentration camp likewise to Temphalenor 13th Red soldiers proceed on leave UK prior to deluvy to	

WAR DIARY
or
INTELLIGENCE SUMMARY

Army Form C. 2118.

Sheet 3

(Erase heading not required.)

Place	Date	Hour	Summary of Events and Information	Remarks and references to Appendices
MUSCRON	22-24		Res Depot in U.K. for duty.	
			20 OR transferred to 36 Bn Machine Gun Corps.	
			1 OR transferred to Remount Depot Courtrai.	
			(Capt) Rev C.D. Irvine proceeded to concentration camp prior to demobilisation.	
	26		1 OR joined Bn from U.K.	
	27		2 OR proceeded on leave from club to U.K.	
	28		1 OR proceeded to A.O.C. Calais.	
			Lieut C.F. McCauley transferred sick to U.K.	
			No 7734 Sgt J. Meredith awarded Decoration Militaire (Belgian) and Croix de Guerre by Belgian authorities.	
			(Capt) Rev W.F. Anketon M.C. proceeded to Calais to duty.	
	31		6 OR proceeded to concentration camp prior to being demobilised.	

1/2/19.

[signature] Adjutant
1st Bn. THE ROYAL IRISH [REGT?]

Army Form C. 2118.

WAR DIARY
or
INTELLIGENCE SUMMARY.

(Erase heading not required.)

Instructions regarding War Diaries and Intelligence Summaries are contained in F. S. Regs., Part II. and the Staff Manual respectively. Title pages will be prepared in manuscript.

M 55

Place	Date	Hour	Summary of Events and Information	Remarks and references to Appendices
Moscow	April 1st		1st BATTN. THE ROYAL IRISH RIFLES	
			108 joined the Bn.	
			Two Maj(?) Blunt B Sc sent to hospital whilst on number Dr	
	2		30H transf to 13 B Royal Irish Rif	
	9/10		10H trans' to R.E.	
			2nd Lieut ___ to proceed to UK for orderly-room duty – 1 sent	
			10H proceeded to Military Prison Tower	
			Major Afflictor took over command of Battn on 26th inst	
	14		10H on leave	
			Lt Edwards an Struck off that of B on number leave UK	
	16		10H transferred to 12th B Royal Irish Rif	
			10H proceeded to hospital on long term sick	
	22		10H transferred to 12th B Royal Irish Rif	
	23		10H on leave by U.K. Dept – Struck off the strength of Bn	
			20H transferred to 12th B Royal Irish Rif	

30 April 1919

[signature]

WAR DIARY
INTELLIGENCE SUMMARY
(Erase heading not required.)

Army Form C. 2118.

Instructions regarding War Diaries and Intelligence Summaries are contained in F. S. Regs., Part II. and the Staff Manual respectively. Title pages will be prepared in manuscript.

1 R Irish 10 56

Place	Date	Hour	Summary of Events and Information	Remarks and references to Appendices
Moascar.	May 1919			Queried
	5th		1 O.R. to U.K. invalided. Lieut J.J. O'Nullivan taken over command of H.B. Coy. vice Lt. S.M. Jamison. Leave U.K.	
	6th		2 O.R. joined battalion from U.K. 1 O.R. attached from 5th Army Concentration Camp.	
	8th		Temporary Major (acting Lt Col.) J.P. Hunt, D.S.O., D.C.M. to be Temporary Lieut. Col. authority War Office letter No. 111693/8. M.S. 4.B. d/23.4.19.	
	9th		11 O.R. demobilized. Lieut Col J.P. Hunt, D.S.O. & D.C.M. having returned from leave U.K. resumed command of the battalion. 2.5.19. Major G.L. Epperson, M.C., resumes his duties as 2nd in Command. 2.5.19.	
	16th		1 O.R. to 5th Army Concentration Camp. Struck off streng. 7th. 1 O.R. transferred to 12th Bn. Struck off streng. 7th.	
	17th		1 O.R. t̶o̶ t/Capt W.C. Gardiner transferred to 5th Area H.Q. + Struck off the strength of the battalion.	
	19th		Lieut S.H. Jamison took over duties of Act. Adjutantance t/Capt. W.C. Gardiner to H.Q. 5th Area.	

Army Form C. 2118.

WAR DIARY
or
INTELLIGENCE SUMMARY.
(Erase heading not required.)

Instructions regarding War Diaries and Intelligence Summaries are contained in F. S. Regs. Part II. and the Staff Manual respectively. Title pages will be prepared in manuscript.

Place	Date	Hour	Summary of Events and Information	Remarks and references to Appendices
Mouscron	May 1919		1 O.R. Taken on strength rejoined from General Base Depot.	
	21.		1 O.R. Taken on strength and struck off the strength of the battalion.	
	22.		Lieut J.F. O'SULLIVAN transferred to 15th Bn. and struck off the strength of the battalion. Authority 36th Div. No. 25/38/3. 29. of 17/5/19.	
			12. O.R. Transferred to 15th Bn. & struck off strength of battalion.	
			Lt Col. J.J. HUNT D.S.O. D.C.M. assumes command of the battalion.	
	23.		Groups 23/5/19 & is struck off the strength of the battalion vice Major J. Jefferson M.C. takes over command the battalion vice Lt Col. J.J. Hunt D.S.O. D.C.M. to No. 3 Labour Group.	
			Coke (3 Officers and 34 O.R.) and Band (3/O.R.) left MOUSCERON at midday, by train for Dunkirk. Held up at STEENWERCK, by explosion of large ammunition dump. Arrived Dunkirk 'A' Camp at midnight Billeted in huts.	
	24.		Cadre passed through Delousing Camp and moved to No. 3. Embarkation Camp.	
	25-28.		Remained in No. 3. Camp. Dunkirk.	
	28.		Transport loaded on S.S. MOGILEFF.	
	29.		Sailed from DUNKIRK on S.S. MOGILEFF.	

J. Jefferson Major
ADJUTANT
1st BN. THE ROYAL IRISH RIFLES.

29/5/19

www.ingramcontent.com/pod-product-compliance
Lightning Source LLC
Chambersburg PA
CBHW081239170426
43191CB00034B/1986